English Revision
Ordinary Level

Joseph Kelly

Gill Education
Hume Avenue
Park West
Dublin 12
www.gilleducation.ie
Gill Education is an imprint of M. H. Gill & Co.

978 0 7171 8873 4
Design by Liz White Designs
Print origination by Carole Lynch

For permission to reproduce photographs, the author and publisher gratefully acknowledge the following:

© Alamy: 8, 13T, 14, 19, 52, 55, 62, 78, 85, 115CL, 115R; © Collins Photo Agency: 115L, 139; © Dany Pepin: 29; © iStock: 13BL, 13BR, 22, 24, 26, 39, 71, 77, 91, 93, 120, 124T, 143; © Getty Images: 4, 15, 25, 74, 123, 124B, 146; © Penguin Random House: 107; © Rex Features: 115CR; © State Examinations Commission: 1, 5.

Quotes and book cover image from *The Spinning Heart* by Donal Ryan. Published by Double Day. Reprinted by permission of The Random House Group Limited © 2013.
Quotes from *The Handmaid's Tale* by Margaret Atwood. Published by Vintage. Reprinted by permission of The Random House Group Limited, © 2017.
'A Removal from Terry Street' by Douglas Dunn (© 2003, Douglas Dunn) are printed by permission of United Agents (www.unitedagents.co.uk).
'Seagull' by Brian McCabe from *Body Parts* (Canongate 1999). Reproduced by permission of the author.
Extract from *The Real Mrs Brown: Brendan O'Carroll* by Brian Beacom © Brian Beacom 2013. Reproduced by permission of Hodder and Stoughton Limited.
Extract from 'Michael Palin: "Pleasure, pain – it's all there in my diary"' by Michael Palin, published in *The Guardian*, September 2015. Copyright © Michael Palin. Reproduced with permission.

CONTENTS

Acknowledgements

I am indebted to the many students in Meánscoil Iognáid Rís who have inspired much of this book. Also, thank you to my teaching colleagues who continue to support me every day, and to my parents and my personal editor Emily-Anne, for your wisdom and love, I am most grateful.

This book is intended to bring confidence to all Leaving Certificate Ordinary Level students preparing for their English exam. With the right attitude and exam-focused knowledge, results will be maximised.

Exam Outline and Mental Preparation

- To understand the structure of the exam papers.
- To know the breakdown of marks allocated to each section of the course.
- To develop the right attitude to exam revision.
- To improve crucial reading skills.

Structure of the Exam

- Two papers.
- 200 marks each.
- 400 marks in total.

Paper 1

Paper 1 has **two sections**:

Section 1 Comprehending (100 marks)

- **Three reading choices are given**, one of which can be a set of pictures. There will be a common theme to all three texts, although this makes no difference in answering the questions.
- **Read one text and answer the Question A that follows it.** Question A carries 50 marks and is usually broken into three short questions (15 marks + 15 marks + 20 marks).

2019. M.9   2019L002G1EL

Coimisiún na Scrúduithe Stáit
State Examinations Commission

LEAVING CERTIFICATE EXAMINATION, 2019

English - Ordinary Level - Paper 1

Total Marks: 200

Wednesday, June 5 – Morning, 9.30 – 12.20

- This paper is divided into two sections, Section I COMPREHENDING and Section II COMPOSING.
- The paper contains **three** texts on the general theme of SOCIAL MEDIA.
- Candidates should familiarise themselves with each of the texts before beginning their answers.
- Both sections of this paper (COMPREHENDING and COMPOSING) must be attempted.
- Each section carries 100 marks.

SECTION I – COMPREHENDING
- Two questions, A and B, follow each text.
- Candidates must answer a Question A on one text and a Question B on a different text. Candidates must answer only one Question A and only one Question B.
- **N.B.** Candidates may NOT answer a Question A and a Question B on the same text.

SECTION II – COMPOSING
- Candidates must write on **one** of the compositions 1 – 7.

- **Read a different text and answer the Question B that follows it.** Question B also carries 50 marks, but it is usually a longer question inspired by the text. It can be a letter, magazine or newspaper article, talk or speech, blog, diary, report, advertisement, etc.

Question A (50 marks) + Question B (50 marks) = Total for Comprehending (100 marks)

Section 2 Composing (100 marks)

- The Composing section is sometimes called 'the essay question'.
- There are **seven options of compositions** and they are inspired by the three reading choices in Section 1.
- Compositions carry **100 marks**.
- Three or four options will be **narratives**, e.g. 'write a story'.
- Other options are **similar to Question B in Section 1** (e.g. write a speech, report or article) but are longer.

Total for Composing (100 marks)

Paper 2

Paper 2 has **three sections**:

Section 1 Single text option (60 marks)

- Your **teacher chooses a text** (novel or play) to be studied in detail.
- This is the text that you need to be most familiar with for the exam.
- You must answer **three short questions** on specific moments or issues in the story (10 marks + 10 marks + 10 marks = 30 marks).
- You must answer **one longer question** that requires analysis of bigger issues in the story. You will be given three longer questions to choose from and each will carry equal marks. Choose one to answer (30 marks).

Three short questions (30 marks) + one longer question (30 marks) = Total for Single Text Option (60 marks)

Section 2 Comparative study (70 marks)

- Your **teacher chooses two or three texts** (novels, plays or films).
- You **compare the texts** under specific headings or 'modes'.

MODES OF COMPARISON	
2020	**2021**
Social Setting	Theme
Theme	Relationships
Hero, Heroine, Villain	Social Setting

- **Three** such modes are **prescribed** for the exam each year.
- **Two of the three modes will appear on the paper.**
- **Choose one** of the two modes in the exam, **either A or B.**
- Each mode is usually broken into two parts: **Q1 or Q2. Choose one.**
- It is important to read all of these questions carefully and **make a good choice before you write anything.**
- **You will have two questions under the same mode on the texts you have studied.** The marks are usually divided into **30 marks + 40 marks** (70 marks).

Total for Comparative Study (70 marks)

Section 3 Poetry (70 marks)

A Unseen poem (20 marks)

- Usually a short and interesting poem that you read closely.
- Questions follow the poem. Sometimes there are two short questions of 10 marks each. Sometimes there is one longer question of 20 marks.

B Prescribed poetry (50 marks)

- There are 36 poems prescribed on the course.
- The poems are divided into two sections: 20 poems come from a combined Higher/Ordinary Level list and 16 poems come from a list of poems for Ordinary Level only.
- Teachers and students must be clear about which list of poems they will study closely. Revise one list or the other. There is no need to study 36 poems.
- Four poems will appear on the exam paper: two from one list and two from the other. Choose one poem on which to answer questions.
- Questions follow each poem. Typically they involve three short questions of 10 marks each, followed by one longer question of 20 marks.
- The question carrying 20 marks often asks you to be creative in your response, as opposed to simply explaining what the poem means.

A: Unseen Poem (20 marks) + B: Prescribed Poetry (50 marks) = Total for Poetry Section (70 marks)

Grand Total = 400 marks

The Day of the Exam

Traditionally, the Leaving Certificate exam schedule has begun on the first Wednesday after the June bank holiday. You will be given English Paper 1 just before 9.30 a.m. that day. Thousands of students are given the opportunity to have their knowledge, understanding, skills and attitudes assessed and rewarded.

Nerves

- **Nervousness can be a powerfully positive force in pressure situations.**
  Most students will be nervous, but that is not a bad thing! Believe it or not, it is good to be nervous. By using this book, you will learn how to turn nerves into powerful and effective writing.

- **Your body and your brain are ready to perform!**
  Being **nervous** is physiological, which means it is something to do with your body's reaction to a pressure situation. Being **afraid** is different. It is a psychological state, which means that it is in your head. While both are interlinked, the physical signs of nervousness are an indication that you are physically prepared for the challenge.

> **exam focus**
>
> Keep a positive attitude when revising. Try to enjoy the challenge of reading and writing.

  You might experience sweaty palms as you hold your pen, increased heart rate as you await the paper and a funny feeling in your stomach. All of these signs are **normal and healthy**. Remember that anybody who ever achieved anything of great merit felt exactly the same way. Most students in the exam hall will feel this way, too. So don't get upset by being nervous. It is the way most people will feel.

The Three Cs

Clarity

Clarity means being **clear**. It is absolutely essential that you are clear about what the English exam entails and also what each individual question asks of you. Each chapter in this book will begin with a set of **aims**. Examine the aims closely, so that you **know what you are trying to achieve**. Throughout the book, typical questions for each section will be outlined. Sample answers will be provided, along with close detail on how such answers are graded. A timing guide will also be given and key points will be emphasised. All of these elements will ensure that you have clarity.

> **exam focus**
>
> To write well, you need: **CLARITY, COHERENCE** and **CONFIDENCE**. These elements are reflected in the marking scheme.

Coherence

Coherence means **making sense**. Having worked out what each exam question means, the aim is to write coherent answers. Many teachers and examiners will tell you that students frequently fail to **answer the question asked**. Others fail to answer the right number of questions or simply do not **make sensible choices in the exam** itself. If you have worries about spelling and grammar, try to focus on answering the right questions and making sense. You will be rewarded.

Confidence

Every student wants to be confident. It is actually nothing more than **your feelings about yourself. In order to increase your confidence, you must keep reading and practising your writing.** Then what you write, and how you write it, will be greatly improved. Examiners look for answers that show a broad command of English as well as a student's individual way of responding. If you work hard and feel confident, your efforts will pay off.

Having a **positive attitude** is the starting point for getting good grades in your exams.

2019. M.10   2019L002G2EL

Coimisiún na Scrúduithe Stáit
State Examinations Commission

LEAVING CERTIFICATE EXAMINATION, 2019

English - Ordinary Level - Paper 2

Total Marks: 200

Thursday, 6 June – Afternoon, 2.00 – 5.20

Candidates must attempt the following:

- **ONE** question from SECTION I – The Single Text
- **ONE** question from SECTION II – The Comparative Study
- **THE QUESTIONS** on the Unseen Poem from SECTION III – Poetry
- The questions on **ONE** of the Prescribed Poems from SECTION III – Poetry

INDEX OF SINGLE TEXTS

2 The Marking Scheme

aims

- To understand exactly how the exam is marked, through detailed analysis of two comprehension answers.
- To show the link between **content** (what you write) and **style** (how you write).

How the Exam is Marked

Examiners do not mark your work according to their opinion or guesswork. Every answer is marked according to specific headings outlined below.

exam focus

Always aim to write as much as you can in the time allowed, once it is relevant to the question.

> **Note**
>
> Examiners' Assessments appear throughout the book. You will notice that these contain a breakdown of marks awarded. Marking is done by reference to the **PCLM** criteria for assessment:
>
> - Clarity of purpose (P):   30% of the total.
> - Coherence of delivery (C):   30% of the total.
> - Efficiency of language use (L): 30% of the total.
> - Accuracy of mechanics (M):   10% of the total.

Clarity of purpose (30%)

This is explained as 'engagement with the set task', which is a fancy way of asking whether or not you have **answered the question that was asked**. It also means that you must have a **personal, original answer**. You will be rewarded for honesty and for sticking to what the question asks of you. For example, when you are asked if you **like or dislike the Unseen Poem**, the first sentence of your answer should immediately state **whether you like or dislike it**. This should be followed by your reasons and backed up with quotations and support.

Coherence of delivery (30%)

This aspect concerns structure. Have you **constructed your answer in a logical fashion** with statement, quotation and comment? Do you **make sense** from beginning to end? You are expected to deal with one point per paragraph and to have your ideas ordered in a logical sequence. For example, essays should have a clear beginning, middle and end.

Efficiency of language use (30%)

This refers to your vocabulary, your fluency with words and your phrasing of ideas. In simple terms, it is **how** you write, as opposed to **what** you write. You can never have enough practice in this area. Language skills often determine your final grade.

Accuracy of mechanics (10%)

This refers to spelling and grammar, as well as the correct placement of words in sentences. While you won't be penalised for every error, **poor mechanics can have a negative effect on your overall grade.**

	SIMPLE GUIDE	
1.	Answer the question asked	30%
2.	Make sense in your answer	30%
3.	Use good vocabulary and expressions	30%
4.	Spell correctly	10%

NB! – the marking scheme tells examiners that the individual marks for C, L and M cannot be greater than P. What does this mean for students?

Answering the question asked is the most important thing to do in the exam. Focus very closely on what exactly the questions ask you to do.

The most common mistakes made by candidates are:

- writing responses that don't answer the question

OR

- not choosing the correct questions

This is what causes students to lose the most marks every year.

> The **content** of your answer (**what** you write) covers 60% of the total marks in every question. The **style** (**how** you write) counts for 40%.
>
> Observe how each sample answer is marked according to PCLM throughout the book and try to make your own answers more exam-focused!

Sample Questions and Sample Marking

Below is a reproduction of the first comprehension question from the **2016 Ordinary Level Exam.**

- What follows is a **15-mark question from Part A** with a student's answer.
- Then, there is a **50-mark question from Part B** with a different student's response.
- Read the passage and look closely at **how these answers were marked.**
- Before reading the examiner's assessment, **try to work out the mark that you think the student deserves.** See if you are close to the actual mark.

Section One – Comprehension (LC 2016, OL)

Text 3 – Keeping a Diary

This text is an edited adaptation of an article by Michael Palin from *The Guardian* newspaper. Michael Palin is famous as a member of the Monty Python comedy group and for his TV travel documentaries. Here he writes about his experience of keeping a diary for almost fifty years, and offers advice to would-be diary keepers.

1. When I began to keep a diary in April 1969, I could scarcely have imagined that decades of my life would not only be recorded but later published for all to see. I was twenty-five years old when I took a crisp new ring-backed notepad, headed the page '1969', and wrote more in hope than in expectation.

2. I have always been attracted to lists, and the ultimate for any list keeper is to keep a record of what you've done each day; a diary, in fact. All I'd lacked in the past was the will to keep at it. Very little happened on that first day of the new diary, or so it seemed at the time. Yet when I reread my diary entry for Thursday, April 17th, 1969, my diary reminds me that I had David Jason [Del Boy in *Only Fools and Horses*] around for lunch, and took a phone call about a possible new show with John Cleese [Basil in *Fawlty Towers*, Monty Python member]. If I had not kept a diary I would never remember all this.

3. That's the attraction of a diary. It remains in its own time. It reflects only what happened on that particular day. It doesn't flatter and it isn't influenced by what happened later. In that way it's the most truthful record of real life, and that's why I'm so glad I persevered with it.

4. There are times when I've had to drive myself to do it. Times when I had so little time to write that I just jotted down a few notes, but mostly I've tried to approach each morning's entry as a story of the day that has just passed, without limits and without self-censorship. And composing a story a day is not a bad discipline for any would-be writer.

5. I never wrote with the idea of publication in mind. I don't think I even wrote for another reader. Occasionally I would read a piece to my wife, usually to settle an argument about what we had or hadn't done. But the longer I kept the diaries the more I saw them gathering some sort of historical relevance. Something that happened the day before might have little significance at the time, but twenty-five or thirty years later it acquires an extra dimension.

6. Thanks to the diaries I can remember things that I would almost certainly have forgotten. For a diarist, life ceases to be an indistinct blur. Experiences are there in sharp focus; some an immeasurable pleasure, others a profound pain, which is the way life is. This is why diary-keeping is often prescribed as a therapy for those with depression, or those who feel their lives are somehow out of control. I encourage you to do as I did all those years ago; get your own notebook out and write down the year and the day and what happened to you in the last twenty-four hours. And keep on doing it. I try and get down what I can remember in thirty minutes maximum.

7. I've found the diary habit very helpful to my own development as a writer. You have to be able to think clearly and edit as you go. An online blog is fine, but I feel very strongly that it's not the same thing as writing down your own experiences in your own hand, in your own chosen notebook. Handwriting is so much more personal. It expresses your personality. I can tell from mine how I was feeling at the time – sometimes hurried and rushed, sometimes relaxed and expansive.

8. You may find it hard, as I did, to find time to write. You may get discouraged by days when nothing seems to happen. Don't give up. I found that details of what you ate or who you were with or what music you were listening to might seem insignificant at the time, but as the years go by these are the things you, and others, really want to know about. Tastes and circumstances change so fast that it is often hardly believable that this is what we did then, this is how we lived, and this is what we were all worried about. The diarist keeps tabs on us all.

9. Keeping a diary means that all that seeing and hearing, loving and laughing, excitement and embarrassment, gladness and gloom that go to make up a life are not forgotten. In short, a diary blows away the mists of time, and offers your life back to you.

Question A (i)
What do you learn about Michael Palin from reading the above text? Support your answer with reference to the text.

(15 marks)

SAMPLE ANSWER

> I think Michael Palin is a thoughtful person who likes to keep things organised. He is thoughtful because he says that a diary is 'the most truthful record of real life.' He has been keeping records of his daily adventures since 1969 so he obviously enjoys thinking back over each day and then remembering how things went for him many

years later. He is organised, simply because keeping a diary that long takes effort. He says that 'you have to be able to think clearly and edit as you go along.' He sounds like a man who likes things to be clear and simple to follow. That's why he writes a diary that is easy to read afterwards.

(117 words)

NOTES ON THE MARKING SCHEME

- For 15-mark questions, the first two headings (purpose and coherence) are combined, as are the other two (language and mechanics)
- This happens for all questions which have <u>less than 30 marks</u>
- The 15 marks are then divided as follows:
  9 marks for WHAT is written
  6 marks for HOW it is written

EXAMINER'S ASSESSMENT

The student does answer the question asked and provides two quotations with following explanations. At 117 words, including two points with quotation and explanation, this is precisely what a 15-mark answer should read like. The vocabulary provided is of a very good standard and there are no errors in 'mechanics', i.e. spelling and grammar.

MARKS AWARDED

P+C	=	9
L+M	=	6
Total	=	15/15 (O1 Grade)

key point

Effort is rewarded at Ordinary Level. Answer the question asked, as best you can, in the time allowed.

Now look at Question B, which follows.

- You cannot choose the B question from the same text as the A question. A **different student's response is found here.**

- In this case, the four aspects of marking – purpose, coherence, language and mechanics – are divided separately to give a breakdown of **15 + 15 + 15 + 5 = 50 marks.**

- This is the case for all questions which have **30 marks or more.**

exam focus

Students can't choose the B question from the same text as the A question.

Question B

Write an article, to appear either in your school magazine or on your school's website, in which you offer advice to your fellow students on finding a part-time job for the summer holidays. Your advice should include tips about where to find work, how to make a successful application and how to prepare for an interview.

(50 marks)

SAMPLE ANSWER

Hi everyone. Stacy here once again with my monthly update on all things trending and happening in the world of St Mary's. As this is the final instalment before the exams next month, I think it's a good time to put aside all thoughts of June and instead think about the glorious summer of freedom ahead.

There is one major problem however, all that celebrating and partying is going to cost you a pretty penny. And given that most of us are gone beyond pestering our parents for money, now is the time to seriously consider seeking out some part-time work. Getting a job isn't as simple as you might think. And employers expect certain things from you in return. So here are my five key tips to securing a job for the summer.

1) Apply for a variety of jobs. Don't decide beforehand that your only going to work in a pub or an office. It doesn't happen that way. Start with the obvious things like bar or restaurant work, shop assistant, working with a small local business or handing out leaflets for charity. Once you keep applying, something will eventually come your way.

2) Be willing to work hard for little money. This might not sound great but it is the reality. We all have to start at the bottom. Just deal with it. If you want money, then this will mean making sacrifices.

3) Be polite and friendly, but not too much, when speaking to a potential employer. Nobody will employ somebody who gives off a nasty or grumpy air when you meet them. You are young, skilled and enthusiastic so don't be afraid to let that shine in an interview or job application.

4) Always be on time, most especially if you have an interview for a job. If you cannot be on time for an interview it is very likely that you will not be employed as a result. If you get a reputation for being late, taking too many breaks or coming in with a hangover, then you won't last long.

5) Think about how you should dress yourself for the job. Work is not usually an excuse to get dressed up and flaunt yourself, unless you fancy being a part-time model. Working with a horse trainer, for example, might involve a lot of long hours and muck and dirt. If going to the races, then you will be expected to look professional and stylish. But remember that it is the horse, not you, that is the centre of attention. Also, if it is a job that has a specific uniform, like in a restaurant, then bear in mind what this will look like to the customers. You must always try to look professional and tidy.

There are many other things to think about but if you keep these five in mind, you should definitely get work of some kind this summer.

Until next year!

Stacy

(494 words)

EXAMINER'S ASSESSMENT

This is an **excellent** effort. At 494 words, it is **long enough**, addressing the question as required. The **register (language, tone, purpose)** is **appropriate to a school magazine**. This deserves good marks. It is **well-structured**: five different pieces of advice are offered, which is a good way to answer the 50-mark task. **Vocabulary** is of an excellent standard. There are very few **spelling/grammar** errors to note.

MARKS AWARDED

15 + 15 + 15 + 5 = 50/50 (O1 Grade)

Further details of how the English exam is marked can be found at **www.examinations.ie.** Follow the links to the relevant papers.

3 Language Genres in the Exam

- To learn about the different genres of language that appear in the exam.

In studying Leaving Certificate Ordinary Level English, you need to be familiar with five genres:

1. **Informative language:** the language of information.
2. **Narrative language:** the language of story.
3. **Persuasive language:** the language of persuasion.
4. **Argumentative language:** the language of logic.
5. **Aesthetic language:** the language of beauty and style.

- **Informative language** is all around you. It is **direct, factual, objective** and should be **easy to understand.** You will employ lots of informative language in your exam answers.

- **Narrative language** is found in **stories, diaries** and **personal essays.** Not all students who like to tell stories are necessarily good at writing them. (Chapter 5 will help you to make this decision for yourself.)

- **Persuasive language** attempts to put forward a point of view or opinion in a way that might **influence** other people. It is often **emotive.** This means that it touches people's **feelings** more than their logic or sense. It is used in political speeches and is essential in good advertising and various other strands of the media. It is likely that you will use persuasive language in many of your answers.

- **Argumentative language** is the language of logic and argument. It is less concerned with emotive language than with **logical**, **rational** thought and speech. A **debate** is by definition an argument. While argument tries to remain cold and **factual**, persuasion contains more emotion and suggestion. You may find questions in Paper 2 that ask you to argue for or against a viewpoint. The wording of these questions often contains the phrase: 'Do you agree with ...?'

- **Aesthetic language** is found in works of **literature**, such as poetry, drama and cinema. It is considered **beautiful** or **stylish** language and can be called 'aesthetically

These five language genres are all around you every day. The more you read and the more you look, the more you will recognise them.

pleasing'. This quality gives writing its colour, humour, power and vitality.

Recognising the Genres

What follows are **five short passages**, all of which refer to the same concept: a cake. In each case, identify which of the genres is being used.

1. Cakes are an essential feature of most modern wedding celebrations. I would argue that to replace such a standard cake with a jelly and ice-cream monstrosity is illogical and foolish. I also fear that it will cause an unwanted mess due to its likely melting before the main course is finished.

2. Take the cake mixture, already well settled, and place in a non-stick baking dish. Smooth around the edges and ensure that none of the mixture contains lumps. Cover with a baking sheet and place in a preheated oven at 180 degrees centigrade. Cook for two hours, or until the top is golden and crispy. Allow to settle before removing from the dish.

3. The scoop of the spoon, the bend of the bowl. The sweep of mother's hand as she gathers the precious remaining grains of flavour into her cloudy, floury fingers. With a final few stirs and whips, the gluey mixture is ready for its final journey to the cavernous oven. Then the real moment of tension: the split second before mother tosses the utensils to the waiting sink. It is all the time he needs. With an innocent, pleading grin, he gently swipes the sugar-and-dough coated delicacy. Wooden spoons never tasted so good.

4. The day Henry decided to bake his own wedding cake was the day it started to go wrong. While it might seem inappropriate now to blame divorce on such trivial matters, wars have been fought over less. Anyway, Henry was a stubborn type, insisting on an ice-cream monstrosity despite advice from those who knew better.

5. As one who speaks for the marginalised of this society, I implore you all to donate any unwanted cakes for the upcoming charity cake sale. Your company produces more than five hundred cakes a week, some of which end up being thrown out because of a lack of demand from your regular customers. Can you really continue with this thoughtless policy, as others beg for scraps of food to survive? You have the power to bring about change.

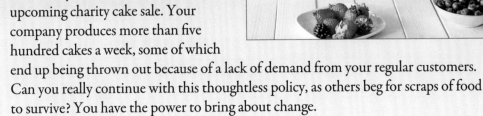

Did you notice the specific features of each genre?

1. **Argumentative** language appeals to logic and sense, e.g. a jelly and ice-cream cake is likely to melt.
2. **Informative** language is mostly factual. In this case, we read the instructions for successfully baking a cake.
3. **Aesthetic** language rises above the ordinary and the purely informative. This beautiful and colourful description of a childhood memory stimulates our imagination.
4. **Narrative** language tells a story, as in the story of poor Henry whose stubbornness gets him into trouble.
5. **Persuasive** language tugs at your feelings, e.g. pleading with the reader to consider the needy in society.

exam focus

If you are familiar with different language genres, you will find it easier to answer questions.

Your teacher has probably helped you become familiar with examples of each genre. In many cases, a piece of writing will contain **combinations** of the above. For practice, re-read Chapter 1 and find examples of each genre.

 # Comprehension

- To examine the **types of questions** that occur in the Comprehension section.
- To understand the importance of **choosing the questions wisely** before answering any of them.

While the Comprehension section appears straightforward, it does amount to **25% of your final total**, so treat it with care.

Comprehension means to understand something. The Comprehension section is a fairly gentle start to your Leaving Certificate, since the questions aim to test your ability to respond logically and creatively to questions on a given text.

Three or four different **extracts** will appear on the exam paper. These will consist of written pieces usually from a magazine, book, newspaper or other source.

There are two types of questions to answer:

- **Question A:** broken into three parts and amounting to 50 marks in total.
- **Question B:** a single question requiring a longer answer and also amounting to 50 marks in total.

You must choose one Question A for one text and one Question B for a different text.

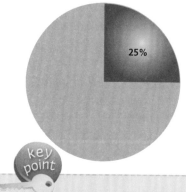

25%

key point

If you choose the *same* text for **Question A and Question B, you are guaranteed to lose at least 50 marks,** which is 12.5% of the total. This can mean a serious drop in your final grade. Do not make this mistake!

How to Approach the Comprehension Section

Take time to **read all of the comprehensions. Choose your Question B first.** This is a more demanding exercise, so you should pick the one you feel best suits you. Then select your **Question A.** The standard is similar across all questions. **Once your choice is made, answer Question A and then Question B.** The most important rule for Comprehension questions is: **answer the question asked.**

Language Genres in the Comprehension Section

Informative language

All of the texts contain information. This is factual, impersonal language. It is not emotive and it speaks directly, e.g. *Hamlet was the Prince of Denmark*. **It is most likely that A questions will ask you to locate specific pieces of information in the given text.**

> **Choose your questions carefully!** Choose Question B, then choose Question A. Once you've made your choice, complete Question A first, then Question B.

Narrative language

This language tells a story. Clearly you need information to tell a story, so there will be some crossover with informative language here. But narration happens in a time and place (setting) and uses words to create situations, images, feelings and reactions. For example: *I will always remember the day that I broke my leg*. **Narration is likely to be found in B questions.**

Persuasive language

Persuasive language often provides a one-sided, opinionated version of events. The main goal of persuasive language is to make the audience **feel** a certain way, by playing on emotions such as fear, excitement, desire, etc. All forms of advertising, for example, use persuasive language, through buzzwords, slogans and colourful phrases, e.g. *8 out of 10 cats prefer it; Unbeatable value at our new store; The time for change has come, etc.* **B questions that involve a talk with an audience, advertisement scripts or political speeches must all involve persuasive language.**

Argumentative language

An argument presents facts in a clear, logical and convincing way. For example: *Uniforms should be compulsory in schools for the following three reasons ...* Each of your A answers should read like a short argument, where you tackle the question by using evidence selected from the text. **Most comprehension exercises involve arguing your point in a logical and clear way.** B questions, such as a debate or journalistic article, are likely to involve argument.

Aesthetic language

All good writing is aesthetically pleasing, even if you don't immediately recognise this quality. But what is aesthetic language? A simple way of understanding this is to ask: **does it sound good to read?** This happens when we write answers as if we were artists enjoying our work, rather than students struggling to succeed.

> 'Students struggling to succeed' is a simple example of alliteration, an aesthetic feature. 'The exam is a marathon' is a metaphor. 'The exam hall is like a pressure cooker' is a simile. All of these features of language show how we can elevate and improve our expression through the use of aesthetics. You can write like this too!

Comprehension: 'A' Questions (50 marks/ 35 minutes)

- These short questions will ask you:
  - **What** is the writer saying?
  - **How** does the writer say it?
  - What is your **response** to it?
- Each question will be marked out of **10, 15 or 20 marks. All the questions in the section will add up to a total of 50 marks.**
- You must **write a little more** and think carefully about any 20-mark questions.
- It is a good idea to read the questions first, **underlining key words** so as to work out the **purpose** of the question.
- This allows your mind to figure out answers **subconsciously** as you read.

Sample Question – 2015 Exam Paper, Text 2

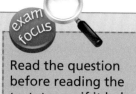

'THE REAL MRS BROWN'

This adapted text is based on edited extracts from **The Real Mrs Brown: Brendan O'Carroll,** *an authorised biography by Brian Beacom. In it we discover the influence of Brendan O'Carroll's mother, Maureen, on his popular sitcom character, Agnes Brown.*

> Read the question before reading the text, to see if it helps you form an answer.

1. Flashback to 17 September, 1911 in Dublin City, Ireland. Seventeen-year-old Lizzie was set to marry Michael McHugh. The pair were madly in love and ready to head to America together to start a new life – but without telling Lizzie's parents. Lizzie's father was deeply against them marrying. When he heard of their romance he attacked Michael, breaking his forearm and collarbone. Michael and Lizzie knew that they had to escape Ireland. That's why they had saved for a year to buy tickets for the long sea voyage. But Lizzie's mother found out about the plan and convinced her husband he had to accept Michael, or he'd lose his daughter forever. Michael and Lizzie's father shook hands and the next day Michael McHugh put an advertisement in the newspaper offering his boat tickets for sale. The ship they would have sailed on was the *Titanic*.

2. Meanwhile, Lizzie and Michael became Mr and Mrs McHugh and a child was born: a baby girl. She was christened Maureen and she was to become Brendan O'Carroll's mother, the woman who provided most of the inspiration for Brendan's sitcom heroine, Agnes Brown. Speaking of his mother, Brendan O'Carroll said, 'People used to ask me if Agnes Brown was based on my mother and I'd say no. But in recent times, I've come to realise just how close they are.'

Indeed. Both are battlers. Both could find a colourful adjective when roused, although Maureen was smarter and way more ambitious than the havoc-creating, uneducated, Agnes Brown. Maureen could definitely deliver a cutting one-liner, just as Agnes does. Maureen could also take a simple tea towel and turn it into a weapon, as Agnes frequently does. Both Maureen and Agnes would lay down their lives for their kids, but loved to make fun of them. Brendan's mammy also had the ability to get what she wanted out of people, just as Agnes can, using the cleverest of psychology, becoming a bit pathetic when required. And if that didn't work, like Agnes, she would tell the world exactly where it was going wrong.

3. Maureen's healthy disrespect for authority – life is to be challenged and rules are there to be broken – is evident in Agnes. As Agnes does, Maureen lived in crowded houses, and managed to create her own safe little world. There are more similarities. Maureen wasn't entirely comfortable with modern devices either. She had little time for small-minded people. Agnes Brown now and Maureen O'Carroll then would be ready and willing to smack the face of injustice.

4. Maureen had incredible energy and studied hard, and her reward was to be sent to University College Galway, a rare achievement for a woman at that time. She became a teacher of languages, and loved her career. But on the day she married Gerry O'Carroll in 1936, she was fired from her job as it was illegal for female teachers in Ireland to be married. Did Maureen O'Carroll take this lying down? 'My mother was a force of nature,' Brendan recalls. 'She said, "I'm not having that!" and joined the union and battled to get that law changed. She shares that feisty, fighting spirit with Agnes Brown.'

5. It wasn't a huge surprise when the Irish Labour Party asked her to run for parliament, Dáil Éireann. But it was a surprise when she won in the General Election of 1954. It was remarkable for a working-class female to achieve that level of success. What made it all the more extraordinary was that she had given birth to nine children. And, in what offers an insight into the character of Maureen O'Carroll, one of her kids, Phil, was adopted.

6. Why does *Mrs Brown's Boys* work? It's Agnes Brown, of course. Every family has one: the busybody, the scathing commentator, the woman with a sharp tongue who can still hug her kids like they are babies.

Question (i)

Based on Maureen O'Carroll's experiences, outlined in the extract above, which word or words from the following do you think best describe the situation experienced by many women in Ireland in the past?

Challenging   Difficult   Unequal

Explain your answer, supporting the points you make by reference to the text.

(15 marks)

SAMPLE ANSWER

I think the words 'challenging' and 'unequal' are two words that describe the situation for women in Ireland in the past. It seems that women were expected to get married and have many children back in the time of Maureen O'Carroll. There was a great challenge in feeding and clothing so many children. She had nine, which is very unusual for today. It is very unequal because she had to quit her job as a teacher. To me that sounds very wrong. It was wrong then and is wrong today still.

EXAMINER'S ASSESSMENT

The candidate chooses two words, but does not adequately expand upon either of them. This answer would be better if the candidate made a **POINT,** by choosing one word and then using a **QUOTATION** to support the choice. It would benefit from have some follow-up **EXPLANATION** or commentary after that. For the full 15 marks, **TWO brief points**, well made, is usually sufficient. This answer is perhaps too brief and lacking development to score highly. The candidate does show some level of **understanding**, however, and the answer is broadly correct. Language and mechanics are **basic but correct**.

MARKS AWARDED

5 + 4 = 9/15 (O4 Grade)

key point

Answers require you to follow the 'POINT-QUOTE-EXPLAIN' formula for each paragraph you write.

Comprehension: 'B' Questions (50 marks/35 minutes)

B questions could be considered 'short essay' questions. These questions test your personal writing skills within a closely defined task. Therefore you must always bear in mind **what the task is.**

key point

Remember this as a golfer would: you are trying to score a **par** on each question. Always know your purpose, audience and register for each question on Paper 1.

Each B question will have:

- A specific **purpose**: what you must write.
- A stated **audience**: to whom the piece is addressed.
- A particular **register**: the piece must sound right.

PURPOSE, AUDIENCE, REGISTER

The **purpose** and the **audience** will be indicated in the question itself. Close reading of the questions will reveal them to you.

However, **register** is more difficult to define. The scenarios below will help you to understand and find the right register:

- Imagine speaking to a small child and explaining something complicated. You will use certain words and phrases and take a gentle tone in order to be understood. You would not speak the same way to an adult about the same issue. You expect that the adult will understand differently, so you change your language and tone to suit the audience.

- Explaining the economic situation to a group of students in university will require lots of factual analysis and statistical data. A politician explaining the economic situation to voters will need a much more careful (and perhaps emotive) approach in order to be understood.

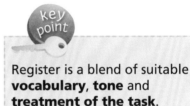

Register is a blend of suitable **vocabulary**, **tone** and **treatment of the task**.

Types of B Questions

By looking at past papers, you will notice that some B questions require similar answers. They can be grouped into types in order to help with revision and practice.

1. Writing for media

Examples include:

- **Review**
- **Newspaper article**
- **Report**
- **Commentary on an event**
- **Advertisement script**
- **Blog.**

This type of question involves writing for the media. Questions can take many forms, but there are overall similarities within the type.

If you like to read newspapers, blog or follow current affairs, a media-type question may suit you. Perhaps there is a journalist or sports commentator inside you waiting to get out! If you like **expressing opinions to a broad audience**, consider this option on the exam paper.

In questions that involve writing for media, there is bound to be lots of opinion. Sometimes **bias** can occur when a writer takes a very one-sided view of a situation. Since this is a creative exercise, a one-sided view could make for very good reading, e.g. a sports commentator with a very strong preference for one team over another can write very entertaining pieces.

SAMPLE QUESTION – WRITING FOR MEDIA, 2019 EXAM

Question

You have been asked by a mobile phone company to produce an **article** for their website, offering guidance on the polite and appropriate use of mobile phones by people of all ages.

The article should include a combination of 'dos and don'ts' in relation to polite and appropriate mobile phone usage. Write the article you would produce.

(50 marks)

SAMPLE ANSWER

Everybody has a phone nowadays. Everybody likes to be seen using their precious device, particularly if it's a new iPhone 11 or the Galaxy S10, or whatever. And because of this, everybody has an opinion on what is the correct and appropriate way to use them. For example, in my view, there is nothing more annoying than sitting near somebody roaring down their phone about how wonderful their life is, while you just want to be left in peace. So maybe I should say the 'polite and appropriate' way to use them because the main issue here is manners and courtesy, not technical know-how. So let me suggest just two 'do's and don'ts' for the polite use of mobile phones.

Dos:

Know your location: Turn on the location tracker on your phone. A shortcut to maps on the home screen might help. Always have your location tracker turned on so that if anything goes wrong, you can be found quickly in an emergency. The location tracker also reminds you that certain phone etiquette is appropriate in particular places. For example, if entering religious buildings or a place with sensitive activities, like a hospital or funeral home, it is best to turn your phone completely off. The location tracker is a useful prompt to be respectful.

Be aware of your ringtone and volume: Having a very loud or annoying ringtone or notification setting is certain to drive friends, family and neighbours crazy. Experiment with these tones (see the tones setting on the device's global settings) and remember that short and quirky is better than loud and obnoxious. People definitely judge others based on their phone's sounds so it is crucial to be aware of which ones to avoid.

Don'ts:

Using the phone at the table: One of the worst habits is using your phone while eating, especially in a restaurant. Flashing the iPhone for a selfie with friends in McDonald's is ok but not if you are on a date or with family. Similarly, don't use your phone when ordering food in a queue or at a till. It annoys everybody and is likely to slow down service while you fumble with your electronic gadget. Just don't do it.

Sticking it in your back pocket: Although we love to see the sort of phones people have (and showing off our own), it is important to keep them secure when not in use. One of the worst places to put a phone is in a rear pocket. It can very easily be snatched. Also, it is likely that you might actually sit on it and damage it, so best to put your device in your bag or inside a coat!

There you are, folks – some basic tips for polite and appropriate mobile phone usage!

(461 words)

EXAMINER'S ASSESSMENT

An excellent attempt: the candidate breaks it into two 'dos' and two 'don'ts', with a beginning and brief ending. Vocabulary is good, especially the verbs used. Light-hearted register and an enjoyable piece to read. The answer is appropriate to the task.

MARKS AWARDED

14 + 14 + 14 + 5 = 47/50 (O1 Grade)

2. Letters and diary entries

These answers must be written with the assumption that very few people, if any, will get to read them. They are often much more **personal** and **intimate** than other forms. Sometimes they can be **formal**, as in a formal or business letter.

If you feel comfortable **expressing your feelings** in a diary, or if you write letters when the opportunity arises, you should consider this type of question. Some people find it **easier to write things down** rather than say them directly to another person. If you are like this, letters and diary entries might be suitable forms for you.

Revise the section on **diary entries** in Chapter 2. Study the example, sample answer and marking scheme there. Below you will find more information on **letters**.

SAMPLE QUESTION – LETTER, 2015 EXAM

Question

You have decided to apply for a weekend job in a pet shop, Wacker's in Donaghmede, Dublin. Write the letter of application you would submit to the Manager of the pet shop.

(50 marks)

SAMPLE ANSWER

23 Ramblers Lane
Swords Road
Co Dublin
19 May 2018

Dear Sir/Madam

My name is Harry Macken and I am 16 years old. I read the advertisement for the job in your store 'Wacker's Pet Shop' in Donaghmede. I would like to apply for this job for the upcoming summer break.

I have some experience working with animals. My uncle Sean has a collection of racing pigeons. I have worked with him for six years in looking after the pigeons and would consider myself quite skilled in dealing with all kinds of birds. I see that you have a large collection of finches, budgies and parakeets in your shop so my experience in this field would be valuable.

We have also had family pets such as dogs, cats and goldfish over the previous years. My mother put me in charge of our pet greyhound when I was 12. Unfortunately, he was run over by a van. Because of this, I am aware of how people can get very close to their pets. I know how upset people get when their pet gets injured or dies. I think this would be very valuable to you in helping people choose the right pet for them.

I am hard-working, well-behaved and willing to work long hours for the money. I get on well with people and I get on even better with animals. I have a kind personality.

I enclose a C.V. which I did in my transition year class in school. The name of my references are at the bottom. I look forward to working with you if you could offer me this job.

Yours sincerely,

Harry Macken

(267 words)

EXAMINER'S ASSESSMENT

The candidate does write a letter and it is set out in the **format and style of one**. The **expression is basic** and to the point while the **vocabulary is adequate**. The answer is quite brief for 50 marks and would benefit from greater emphasis on why the applicant wants the job. Overall, a solid answer, just short of high marks.

MARKS AWARDED

12 + 11 + 11 + 4 = 38/50 (O3 Grade)

3. Speeches and talks

These questions are for you if you can imagine yourself before an audience delivering a powerful speech or informative talk. If you have watched great **public speakers** such as politicians and leaders delivering speeches, copy their approach in your writing. Remember a time when you saw your school principal or another teacher give an **informative talk**. Perhaps you have experienced great team-talks given by **sports coaches** or mentors. Can you do the same in your writing?

In these answers, you are aiming to be both **informative** and **emotive**: you want people to understand you, but you also want them to **feel a certain way**.

SAMPLE QUESTION – TALK OR SPEECH, 2017 EXAM

Question

Your school principal has asked you to give a **talk** to Third Year students who are about to choose their Senior Cycle subjects.

In your talk you should explain to the students **why it is important to make good decisions** when choosing subjects for their Leaving Certificate course and suggest what you think they should consider when making these decisions.

(50 marks)

SAMPLE ANSWER

'Good afternoon, my fellow students. You know me as Smiley, the nickname I got in First Year, which has stuck with me ever since. Thanks, classmates! But my full name, as some of you know, is Sarah-Jane Murphy, and I am delighted to speak to you as you come near the end of the Junior Cycle. Our principal, Ms Moynihan, has asked to me tackle the question of choosing your subjects before heading into the Senior Cycle.

To start with, I should say that I have made some poor decisions around my own subject choices. When I was in Third Year, aged 15 and still quite self-conscious, I thought I knew my own mind. It is easy to just follow your initial feelings when it comes to choosing your subjects. Always remember, however, that there are other people who have more experience and knowledge than you. And that is where we all need to start.

When it comes to subject choice, the first key point is to always heed advice from the teachers who want the best for you. If you are being advised to choose one subject over another, be sure to listen. It might not seem obvious but your teachers often know what your strengths are and they genuinely care about your future.

Secondly, be wary of following what your friends are doing. That might sound odd, especially since I'm telling you to follow your teachers instead! You will be a very different person in about two or three years, and Senior Cycle is so much broader and challenging than school up to now. Make choices that suit you, not your friend group. If you are worried about losing friendships, remember that real friends will always be there for you, no matter your choice. New experiences await you so don't let your friend group influence your decision.

Thirdly, we always get told that we should do what we enjoy – it is such an over-used phrase, but of course it is true. Why focus on languages or music, if you don't actually enjoy them? Why not science, even if nobody in your family has done it before? Why not be the pathfinder in your family and become the great scientific genius that you have dreamed about as a little girl in primary school? If you enjoy exercise and sport, then give the sciences a go. Stick to the task, pass your exams and you never know; you might just go on to become that Olympic shot-putter or part of an All-Ireland winning team! It all starts with making good choices. Go for the subject that makes you happy, regardless of any stereotypes it may have. Remember that in a few years, this school life will fly past you and a new phase of your life will begin.

If you consider this advice, even in a small way, I think you will be on the way to making better choices for your future.

Thanks to all for listening and I hope Ms Moynihan is pleased that I got through this without smiling too much!'

(515 words)

EXAMINER'S ASSESSMENT

A high-scoring effort as the candidate has broken it into three specific pieces of advice, around an excellent introduction and conclusion. The advice itself is simple, but the phrasing and word choice is excellent. Very easy to read and understand, having addressed the task at hand.

MARKS AWARDED

15 + 15 + 15 + 5 = 50/50 (O1 Grade)

4. Visual texts

Some students are more comfortable answering a question that is based upon a picture or a set of 'visuals' that appear on the exam paper. When analysing a visual, some basic points must be kept in mind.

Context

The well-known 'w' questions apply here: **where, when, who, why** and **what**. They give us a sense of what the picture is about. Try to guess the context when you first look at the visual.

Purpose

Context will go some way towards understanding the **purpose** of the visual. The picture has been taken for a reason. Guess what that reason might be.

Point of view

From what angle do we see the picture? Is it close-up, long-distance, high-angle, low-angle, hidden, panoramic (seeing everything at once), etc?

Framing

What is in the picture frame? Certain details are included and certain details are left out. Consider elements such as: background, foreground, left, right, centre, corners, middle, positioning, etc.

Colour

Colour affects the way you feel about a picture.

> **key point**
>
> When responding to visual texts, **imagine being in the picture**.

- Bright colours such as yellows and oranges suggest happiness. Red can signify power, danger and adventure.
- Blue is the universal colour for calm. However, it can also suggest unhappiness ('the blues').
- Green is usually the colour for health and the environment. It is especially connected to Ireland and Irishness.
- Black and white visuals can suggest a particular atmosphere or capture a particular time. Remember context here: try to work out why the picture is in colour or black and white.
- Black and white visuals ask you to look more carefully at specific elements like shape and texture. They are also excellent for portraying facial expressions or capturing an event from the past.

The comprehension questions that accompany visual texts will ask you to **interpret or respond to what you see in the picture**.

You could follow the **statement–quotation–comment** approach that many teachers encourage in their classes:

- **State** what you see.
- **Quote** by mentioning specific details in the picture.
- **Comment** by backing up your view.

In recent exam papers, students have been asked to pay close attention to the 'visuals' that are found with the comprehensions. It is unknown whether you will be asked a question worth 10, 15 even 50 marks. However, a question of some sort is quite likely. Here is a sample question and answer based upon a visual from the 2018 exam. It is worth 15 marks.

SAMPLE QUESTION: VISUAL COMPREHENSION QUESTION, 2018 EXAM

Question

Look at the image that appears below. Outline **two or more reasons** why you do or do not think this poster is effective in communicating a message against child labour. Support your answer with reference to both the words and images in the poster

(15 marks)

SAMPLE ANSWER

When I look at this poster, straight away I see a young girl being asked to lift a very heavy load. I feel great sympathy for her as there is no way she should be doing that kind of heavy work and she is probably not being paid very much for it. The fact that the word 'child' is written on her clothes emphasises the fact that she is too young to be working. Also, the way that the words are crossed out on the poster except for the word 'work' is interesting. Young people take things like family, friends and health for granted so it is a good way of communicating the message against child labour. I like the way it is presented in black and white because these colours don't create a positive mood, in fact they create the opposite so this is another reason why it is communicating the message against child labour.

(162 words)

EXAMINER'S ASSESSMENT

Three particular reasons are offered here and the candidate does pay attention to detail. However, the question asks whether the poster is 'effective' and the answer fails to address that. It is is more focused on description and therefore, it would lose some marks. Language is adequate and the sentences are clearly phrased.

MARKS AWARDED

5 (P+C) + 4 (L+M) = 9/15 (O4 Grade)

Answer Formats for B Questions

There is quite a variety in the B questions that could appear on your exam paper. Below are some pointers for different formats you might use in your answers.

Newspaper articles

- **Read, read, read!** There is no substitute for reading newspapers regularly.
- **Tone:** When writing a newspaper article, decide immediately what the tone should be. Do you want it to be sincere, serious, light-hearted, sarcastic, angry, etc?
- **Headlines:** Tabloids tend to be more sensationalist than broadsheets, e.g. 'JAIL THE EVIL BEAST' as opposed to 'Killer to be sentenced tomorrow'. Tabloid headings can be very memorable. When Glasgow Celtic were beaten by Inverness Caledonian Thistle (a much smaller football team nicknamed 'Cally') the following headline appeared in a tabloid and reminded many people of *Mary Poppins*: 'SUPER-CALLY-GO-BALLISTIC-CELTIC-ARE-ATROCIOUS!!!'
- **Opening sentences:** All journalists are skilled at making an impact with their opening sentence.
- **Paragraph length:** Newspapers stick rigidly to one point per paragraph; words are not wasted.
- **Structure:** The most important information is placed at the start of the article. Lesser details are edited out or left to the end. This is called the 'upside-down pyramid' approach because readers frequently read only the start of an article.
- **Quotation:** Journalists use quotation carefully. When they are not sure of an exact quote, they paraphrase or use phrases like 'a source has indicated' or 'reports suggest that', etc.
- **Passive voice:** This means that an article should be written as if from a distance. The journalist does not let 'I' get in the way. They are not telling a story in the narrative sense; they report on what happened. For example: 'A bomb **was found** yesterday', rather than '**I heard** that there was a bomb'.

Reports

- Reports must be **factual** and free from excessive emotion.
- You could be asked to report on a traffic accident, sports event, talent show, report to a committee at the end of the year, etc.
- The most important thing to consider when writing a report is your **audience**. Who are you reporting to?
- Reports must be very **informative**.

Commentaries

- This question comes up occasionally. If you can copy the style of commentaries you hear on radio or TV, this is a possible choice.

- Commentaries require lots of emotion to communicate the excitement of an event. You will need to include some narration and information, but aesthetics should be your ultimate goal. Bring colour to the scene!
- Avoid cliché.
- Similar to tabloid newspaper headings, puns feature in commentaries:

  'It's snow joke: the race is being abandoned!'

  'It looks like curtains for Vladimir Karpets!'

  'John Carpenter nails his opponent!'

  'Woods is definitely in the trees!'

  'Keane to play no longer.'

  Try to include some funny puns in commentaries that you write.

Advertising

- This is all about selling and the clever use of images (in your case, words) to encourage people to buy a product.
- Information and persuasion are on show here.
- An advertisement needs a **slogan**: a catchy phrase to gain attention. Sometimes slogans are funny or even shocking.
- **Memorable information**: Advertisements use scientific or technical language, but they keep it to a minimum.
- **Buzzwords** include: 'best', 'unbeatable', 'superior' and 'a must'. Emotive sentences could be: 'Good parents always ...'; 'Never, ever do ...'; 'Could you possibly not ...'; and 'You would be mad not to ...'.
- **Repetition** is vital for product and brand recognition. Keep mentioning the product or the brand by name or by its benefit or result.

Talks

- In many ways, this is the least formal of all the writing exercises in the exam.
- Once again, you must consider your audience.
- It is likely that this question will ask you to write a talk to be given to some of your **peers** or **colleagues**. Therefore, use the register (vocabulary, tone, purpose, etc.). that you would use when speaking to peers or friends. Practise this in class.
- When writing informal content, it is still important to avoid excessive **slang** or phrases that are too casual, vague or loose.

exam focus

Choose the Comprehension B Question that you like most by determining the task involved and the type of writing that is required.

- like • really • kind of • sort of • yeah • nah • mate • dude • bud

5 Composition

- To analyse the **types of questions** that are found in the Composition section of the exam.
- To demonstrate the key differences between **story** and **discussion** questions.
- To understand the importance of **planning** in this section.

- The Composition section accounts for 25% of the entire exam.
- This part of the exam will take you about **80 minutes** in total.
- Aim to write anything from **700 words upwards**.
- However, the old saying of '**quality not quantity**' applies here.
- Quality essay writing is dependent on good planni so this aspect is covered in detail later on in this chapter.

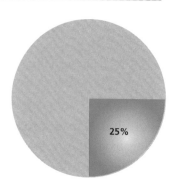

25%

Breakdown of the Composition section:

- The paper contains **seven** composition titles.
- Students choose **one**: worth **100 marks** in total.
- Exam papers from the last number of years reveal that the titles given allow for a choice between a type of **story** and a type of **discussion**, or a combination of both.
- There is sometimes an option to write a **personal essay** based on the visuals in the Comprehension section in Paper 1. Pay attention to the visuals when reading the questions.

key point

If you want to write a talk, speech or article for your Composition, use the guidelines in Chapter 4 for Comprehension B questions. However, remember that your **Composition answer must be longer**!

PAST COMPOSITION QUESTIONS

2019

1. Write a **short story** about a character whose determination to be the centre of attention has unexpected consequences.

2. Write a **personal essay** in which you discuss at least three aspects of life that are considered unremarkable in 2019 that you think may appear strange or remarkable to people in the future.

3. Write an **article**, for publication in a music magazine, in which you describe your ideas for the perfect music festival. The article should deal with the venue, the line-up and the facilities available to festival-goers.

4. Write a **personal essay** in which you discuss what you think your life would be like if you were unable to use any form of social media for a whole year.

5. Write a **short story** in which a group of childhood friends form what becomes a world-famous band but live to regret their success.

6. Write an **article**, to be published in a popular magazine, on the value of volunteering with at least one sporting or charitable organisation. The article should discuss the possible benefits for the people who volunteer their time and energy, and for the organisation(s) involved.

7. Imagine you are representing Ireland at a United Nations conference on the future. Write a **speech**, to be delivered at the conference, in which you discuss both the opportunities and responsibilities facing humanity as we explore space and planets beyond the Earth.

2018

1. Write a **speech**, to be delivered to your classmates, in which you outline the impact, both positive and negative, that technology has on your life. Your speech can be serious or amusing or both.

2. Write a **short story** in which confusion arises because the two central characters, brothers or sisters, are identical twins. Identical twins are twins who look exactly alike.

3. Write an **article** for a magazine popular with young people, in which you outline what you think you, and young people generally, could do to help build better lives for people in your community, and in the world generally.

4. Write a **personal essay** in which you discuss the importance of at least three of the following in your life: family, friends, health, school, fun and work.

5. Write a **short story** which involves a race against time to prevent a disaster.

6. Write a **personal essay** in which you discuss what you have already achieved in life and what you hope to achieve in the future.

7. Write a **personal essay** in which you share your thoughts on the subject of having or not having brothers or sisters.

2017

1. Write a **short story** which features a character who gets into trouble because of his or her sense of humour.

2. Imagine that you have been selected as the Student of the Year in your school and have been asked to deliver a **speech to the staff and students at a school assembly**. The topic for your speech is 'My School Days'. Write the speech, which may be serious or humorous or both, that you would deliver.

3. Imagine you find a box of items from your childhood in your parents' attic. Write a **personal essay** in which you identify what you find in the box and describe the feelings and memories these items evoke for you.

4. Write a **short story** in which a family comes to regret adopting a robot.

5. You have been asked to write an **article for a magazine** popular with young people. In your article you should give advice to Leaving Certificate students on how to develop their study skills, maintain a healthy lifestyle while preparing for exams, and balance study with the more social aspects of life.

6. Write a **personal essay** giving your views on the importance of praise and encouragement as we go through life.

7. Imagine you are a robot teacher. Write at least **three diary entries** in which you record your impressions of humans in general, write specifically about your work as a teacher and give your views on the behaviour of the students that you teach. Your diary entries may be humorous or serious or both.

Once you have chosen your question, you will most likely be writing one of the following types of composition:

- Short story.
- Personal essay: A story or discussion based on your own experience. The 'I' voice is important here.
- Talk or speech to an audience.
- An article of some sort, e.g. newspaper, magazine, blog, etc.

Spend some time browsing these and other essay titles. Make a note of the titles you would prefer and those you would prefer to avoid. This is the first step in choosing a title and properly planning your essays.

The Composition question is sometimes referred to as the 'essay question'. Some students are intimidated by the thought of writing such an essay. It may indeed be the longest piece of continuous writing you have ever written. Over the years, some preconceived notions about the Composition question have taken hold. Let's tackle them here.

1. **'You can write a short story or essay without any planning.'**
   False

   A certain amount of imagination and creativity is needed here. But it is also very difficult to do this question without some sort of plan beforehand. Spider diagrams, mind maps, scribbled notes or whatever suits you will definitely help in creating the final product in the exam. Practise this beforehand; also spend about 10–15 minutes in the exam itself planning what you will write. This is time well spent. It will give structure or shape to your answer. This is what examiners are looking for. **It is obvious that planning and practice before the exam is vital.**

2. **'Writing a story is always the best option.'**
   False

   This issue is of huge significance. While it may seem easy to write a story, other options such as a speech, magazine article or personal essay may suit certain candidates better. If you are not a good storyteller, you will still have plenty of options on the day.

   It is important that you work with your teacher to determine if you have adequate storytelling skills. Otherwise, avoid the short story options and concentrate on something else. Look back over some Leaving Certificate short stories and see if they inspire you to write your own story.

3. **'The essay will decide if you get an A grade or not, or if the examiner will pass or fail you.'**
   Partly true

   Given that this question comprises 25% of the entire exam, it does have a major bearing on your overall grade. However, it is marked according to strict criteria and examiners are trained to look for particular qualities and features. They are not out to judge your opinions or views; they need to examine your language skills.

4. **'Personal, unique, original essays get automatic A grades.'**
   False

   Perhaps you have heard of some famous O1 essays, such as the one entitled 'Creation', where a candidate drew a map of the world. Or an essay entitled 'Why?', for which the candidate wrote 'Why not?' Or best of all, the one about 'Bravery', which inspired a bright student to hand up four blank pages. What grade did they all receive? Such efforts obviously get zero! A good student will aim for anything from **700 words upwards**, which amounts to roughly **two and a half or three A4 pages at a bare minimum.**

5. **'You can learn off an essay and twist it to suit any exercise.'**
   Possible – But not at all advisable

Some teachers have suggested this approach. However, there is the possibility that the student will fail to answer the question asked, which is one of the main reasons for poor grades in English. Unoriginal, 'learned-off' essays do not score well. You can, of course, use an essay plan or outline that went well for you during the year, provided that you follow what the essay question asks of you in the actual exam.

6. **'The Composition is the most important question of the entire exam.'**
   Partly true

Again, with 25% on the line, this is an area to which students must devote time and practice. It is also worth reminding you that no amount of practice and preparation can account for simply writing a bad essay on the day. However, if you make some good choices and write to your full potential, you should be fine.

key point

It's all in the plan!

Option 1: A Short Story

Planning

Here is an old piece of advice: 'Rule number one for making chicken soup is to catch the chicken!' The same applies to writing a short story composition. Catch the chicken by making a **sensible, coherent plan:**

- **Underline key words and jot down ideas.** This applies to all questions on the paper, but the composition is mostly about **your own ideas and expression**, so try to think broadly about the topic once you have underlined the key words.

- **Spend at least 15 minutes planning the detail.** All planning begins with **brainstorming**. It can take the form of spider diagrams or mind maps – whatever way you can comfortably get your thoughts on the page. You may scribble single words or draw diagrams; it really does not matter once you have a way of doing it. Then connect the ideas by following the pointers below.

- The **narrative voice** of a story is important. Pick one of these options:
  1. I am in the story, telling it. This is a **first person narrative.**
  2. I am outside the story, telling it. An 'all-seeing' narrator is used in a **third person narrative.**

exam focus

Remember that first person narratives don't have to be true to life. Invent a story about yourself. You can be anybody!

Key ingredients for a good short story

- Have a **small number of characters**: two or three characters with one main character or **protagonist**. When planning, create a quick profile of each character, listing gender, age, features, etc.
- Give each personality **one strong trait**, such as aggression, impatience, humour, an unusual talent, unique features, etc.
- Work within a **narrow timeframe**. The hub of your story could take place in a few hours or one single day, with a significant episode.
- Include **dialogue** and interaction. Use these elements to suggest details to the reader, e.g. the setting, time and location.
- In order to interest your reader, there must be a challenge, obstacle or **conflict** that the main character must overcome. All good stories contain conflict.
- There must be **tension** or uncertainty before your conflict is resolved. Situations in real life rarely run smoothly; when they do, they make for boring stories.
- Know the **ending** before you begin.
- Understand the purpose of stories. Aim to entertain and **engage** the reader. If the story bores you, it will bore the reader, too.
- Remember the **audience** for your story. In this case, it will be the examiner.
- Do not be at all inhibited or shy about expressing yourself. Speak from the well of your own experiences. Be creative!

Bad planning

To demonstrate how things can go wrong without a plan, read the following passage from a student who chose Question 2 from the 2006 exam. It asks for a short story ending with the sentence: 'What a relief!' The student wrote the entire essay without any planning. So many problems are demonstrated in just this opening paragraph. See if you can identify these weaknesses yourself before reading the analysis overleaf.

What a relief!

Five best friends spent months planning their dream vacation trying to find the perfect place with a mixture of nights out, a relaxing atmosphere during the day and a place you would only go once in a lifetime. John was a typical teenager and loved nothing more than going out with his friends. He was tall and strong and a gym fanatic. He was nineteen years old. John's four best friends were the same age as him and they were friends since playschool. Despite what most people thought, John's friends were not as bad as they seemed. They were party animals and always went out any chance they had, drinking and taking as much drugs as they could get into them. They decided to go to Bangkok in Thailand for six weeks.

Analysis of sample paragraph

This opening paragraph reads like an essay disaster waiting to happen.

- In a short story, you have little time to develop characters. Choose two or three at most. This student has included **far too many characters** for a short story composition.

- Try to avoid **common names** like John or Mary. Go for something more memorable.

- **Personalities** are important. Why does John have to be a 'typical teenager'? Surely it is more interesting to read about a character that is unusual or unique. Also, few nineteen-year-olds fit the bill as 'typical teenagers'.

- Timeframe is crucial. This paragraph suggests that the action will cover a total of six weeks. This is **far too long a timeframe** for this kind of composition. It is better to write short episodes covering a day in the life – even a few minutes in the lives – of a small number of characters.

- The **content** is rather clichéd. The story of five young males heading to Thailand for six weeks has been told so many times. Given the title, it is quite likely that the boys will: have a brush with the law; dabble in drink, drugs, sex or a combination of them all; and somehow escape with their lives only to exclaim, 'What a relief!' This storyline is unoriginal, predictable and lacks imagination. If it was a film, you wouldn't bother watching it.

- Other storylines that are overdone include:
  - **Scoring the winning goal in a football final.**
  - **Waking up to discover that 'it was all a dream'.**
  - **Describing complicated intimate relationships between boyfriends and girlfriends.**
  - **Killing off the narrator at the end. This seldom makes sense in the context of a story.**
  - **Any type of clichéd, overused storylines involving: drinking, drugs, parties, pregnancies, the police, etc.**

While there might be some merit in these subject areas, the problem is that they tend not to be very interesting or **original.** Examiners feel that they have heard all of these stories before and so they will not score them highly in the exam. Therefore, **don't write about them**, unless the question specifically asks you to.

- Given the title, the ending for this story is of huge importance. In fact, **the ending is crucial in all stories** and students should know the end before they begin to write. This title suggests a happy ending: John probably escapes with his life. But perhaps the final

exam focus

Include any rough work or planning you did with your answer booklet. Examiners do take note of this material.

phrase could be the words of the police-chief in Thailand who is delighted to put John behind bars for his drug-trafficking crimes. It is up to you to determine the ending. Just make sure you decide on it before you begin to write.

- We have examined the **content** problems with this sample paragraph. However, there are also **style** issues to be considered. **How** the story is written (vocabulary, sentence structure, grammar, etc.) accounts for another 40% of the marks. Clearly there are style problems in this sample paragraph also: the **opening sentence** is too long; the **vocabulary** is limited; and overall there is not much to recommend it.

> **key point**
>
> The opening paragraph is the most important paragraph to get right.

SAMPLE SHORT STORY

exam Q

Question 1

Write a short story which features a character who gets into trouble because of his or her sense of humour.

- This was the essay title no.1 on the 2017 paper. It is a straightforward concept that presents lots of imaginative potential.
- Many of us can relate to this concept. Think of a real life story where this happened.
- Plan your essay by brainstorming or using mind maps or diagrams to work out how your story will develop.

> **key point**
>
> If an essay title immediately sticks out as being familiar or close to your own personal experience, then it is likely a good choice in the exam.

Here is a sample brainstorming diagram:

Brainstorming

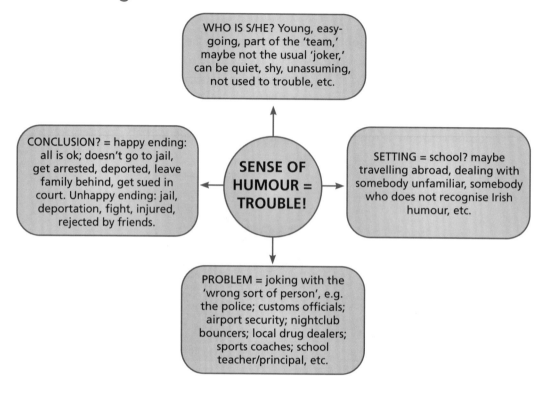

WHO IS S/HE? Young, easy-going, part of the 'team,' maybe not the usual 'joker,' can be quiet, shy, unassuming, not used to trouble, etc.

CONCLUSION? = happy ending: all is ok; doesn't go to jail, get arrested, deported, leave family behind, get sued in court. Unhappy ending: jail, deportation, fight, injured, rejected by friends.

SENSE OF HUMOUR = TROUBLE!

SETTING = school? maybe travelling abroad, dealing with somebody unfamiliar, somebody who does not recognise Irish humour, etc.

PROBLEM = joking with the 'wrong sort of person', e.g. the police; customs officials; airport security; nightclub bouncers; local drug dealers; sports coaches; school teacher/principal, etc.

Short Story – Outline

Having spent 5–10 minutes brainstorming on blank paper, you should now put together the 'shell' of your story. It should have a defined setting, in a time and place, have a clear beginning, middle and end and a sense that a short time passes. It should be realistic enough and you absolutely **must** know how it will end before you start writing.

Here is a suggestion:

> As a group of friends are returning from a trip to America, one of them tries to joke that he has a bomb in his hand luggage. This does not go down well at all and only after being questioned by airport police are they let go home. But they miss their flight and the friends are not entirely happy.

Beginning/Introduction

'Show', don't 'Tell'

Your opening paragraph is vital. It is better to 'hint' and 'suggest' at a time and place, rather than just listing details.

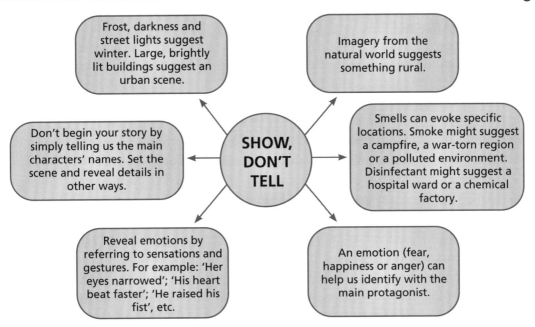

Frost, darkness and street lights suggest winter. Large, brightly lit buildings suggest an urban scene.

Imagery from the natural world suggests something rural.

Don't begin your story by simply telling us the main characters' names. Set the scene and reveal details in other ways.

SHOW, DON'T TELL

Smells can evoke specific locations. Smoke might suggest a campfire, a war-torn region or a polluted environment. Disinfectant might suggest a hospital ward or a chemical factory.

Reveal emotions by referring to sensations and gestures. For example: 'Her eyes narrowed'; 'His heart beat faster'; 'He raised his fist', etc.

An emotion (fear, happiness or anger) can help us identify with the main protagonist.

Have a read of this opening paragraph:

> I don't like airports at the best of times. There is something about the waiting around, the crowds, the over-priced food and the hustle and bustle that just wears me out. Yes, I love the adventure of travelling, the excitement of seeing friends and relatives abroad, the thought of unexplored lands to be conquered. It's the getting through the airport bit that I dread most. Plus, it's hard enough having to mentally deal with things like bombers and terrorists on the news every night. So when Shane decided for some ungodly and outrageous reason to start some funny small talk with the pretty security guard, I knew we were going to be here for a bit longer than usual.

At this stage, we have:

- Setting (airport)
- Characters: narrator, Shane, security guard (this is enough)
- Problem/Obstacle (trouble with security)
- Lots of possibilities from which to develop the story

Middle/Main body of the story

We now need to engage the reader/examiner with some character details. Given the time constraints of the exam, we can't tell the whole life story of anybody – so choose some strong trait that will make the character interesting.

Example: Shane = **confident, funny, amusing**. Likes to entertain people. This is what causes the problem.

SAMPLE PARAGRAPH

I have been friends with Shane since he first moved to the countryside when he was nine. He was quirky, quick-talking and full of mischief from the start. His father and mother had separated so he went to live with his grandparents for a few months to help him cope. They lived about fifty miles south of Belfast City, just over the old border in what is County Monaghan, right next to our family farm. 'Patrick Kavanagh Country' they called it with its stony, grey, drumlin soil. It may as well have been a different continent to a lad like Shane, who knew nothing but life in a terraced West Belfast row of red-brick houses. I suppose he became a comedian to try to offset the usual turmoil that young kids go through. His quick-fire commentary lit up many a boring day in the two-room primary school, once his mother moved full time to live with him the following autumn. But enough of the pop psychology: Shane and I were now stuck in JFK Airport, awaiting what we were told was 'homeland security protocol' after one-joke-too-many from dear old Shane.

At this stage:

- We now know more about the characters and their relationship.
- We are heading towards a climax or turning point or 'key moment' that needs to be resolved.
- We are continuing to 'hint' and 'show' the reader our story – details are gradually revealed.
- We need **dialogue** to take the story further.

Sample paragraph – using dialogue

It is best to end this story on a positive note, otherwise it will be too long and involve too many extra characters, i.e. security guards, lawyers, embassy officials, parents, etc. To keep it simple, we will imagine the discussion that might occur between Shane, the narrator (whose name will be revealed in the dialogue) and an airport security official, as they are being released from custody.

My cheap, two-dollar plastic watch was holding up better than me and reminded me that we were now four hours here and our flight long gone. The door marked 'Airport Security – No Unauthorised Entrance' suddenly swung open and a grim-faced Shane strode out awkwardly, rubbing his wrists as he did so.

'Those wee handcuffs were pure unnecessary,' he whispered to me as we stood together, 'and too tight for my liking. Think I'm some kinda wacko bomber nutjob or something. Pure madness.'

Before we could exchange any more particulars, an equally grim-faced security guard interrupted us as she swished through the door just behind Shane. It was then that I noticed her name tag: **Julia Alvarez – Department of Homeland Security**. Christ, for a moment I thought I was in a TV show.

'Ok you guys, I know Irish people can be funny,' she began in a sharp, pointed tone, 'but in the United States, all persons suspected of, or known to be accomplices of known enemies to the peace of this nation, or any other freedom-loving country, is given the level of attention necessary to establish their likeliness to do harm to themselves or others while in the country. We don't make jokes about being bombers or terrorists. Do you understand the seriousness of the situation here?' I was exhausted trying to work out what that long sentence actually meant. But I think the penny had dropped with Shane.

'Yes, Julia ... I mean Miss Alvarez, I sure do,' he nodded solemnly, trying not to wink at her as he was fond of doing. 'I was only having a wee laugh, pulling yer ould leg if ya know what I mean.' She apparently did not enjoy the thought of an 18-year-old sunburnt, Irish Paddy pulling her leg or indeed anybody else's. I intervened on our behalf.

'Thank you, Miss Alvarez. Shane is a good friend of mine. I know him for years and we have never been in any trouble whatsoever. You can check that with the authorities in Ireland.' I'm sure she had already. I was putting on my very best innocent, wide-eyed altar-boy face. She still wasn't impressed.

'Well, thank you, Mr Callahan, but we have looked into both your affairs and thankfully you appear to have a clean record.' It was the first bit of relief I had felt that evening. But Julia wasn't finished: 'For now!' she added gravely, with a sullen stare at Shane.

Concluding paragraph

Since this is a positive ending, we want something to tie it together, to have something that the examiner will see merit in.

We were handed back our passports, our luggage was thrown at our feet and with that, we were free to go again. No longer suspected terrorists with bombs in our luggage but just two teenage Irish lads again, heading home from our weekend break to New York, courtesy of Aunt Mary living in Queens. But Julia Alvarez had the last word:

'Mr Callahan. Ah, is your name really Harry Callahan?' The question made me pause for a second. Of course it was my name. Did she think I was on a fake passport now or what?

'Yes. That's my name. Is everything ok?' I enquired nervously.

'It's fine. Ya know, maybe you should head to San Francisco next time. You can tell them Dirty Harry is back. They might actually find that funny.'

For the first time she actually smiled. Shane, not being much of a movie fan, shrugged his shoulders, lifted his bag and strode off towards the terminal, a free man once again. I was glad to follow. This time, we were both keeping our mouths shut.

- This conclusion reveals the narrator's full name.
- It is a light-hearted ending to a serious scenario.
- We can see differences in each of the characters' attitudes at this point of the story.
- It ties up the plot in a short timescale and involves a limited number of characters.
- Dialogue is used once more to make the story sound realistic.

Option 2: A Personal Essay

The personal essay asks you to write about an experience you had. Thankfully, it involves **planning** that is broadly similar to the short story. The main difference is that it is expected to be more **sincere** than an imaginative story.

You must be wary of some common pitfalls. Students sometimes write about experiences that are simply not very interesting. Or sometimes they express an opinion that is not thought out fully or is badly informed, in spite of their personal experiences. Examples of themes that are sometimes poorly dealt with include racism, world politics and relationships.

Improving the personal essay option

You should follow all of the advice given for planning a story. When you read an essay title, ask yourself if you have knowledge or experience of it. Do you hold strong opinions on the topic? **If you are unsure, don't choose this particular essay title.**

Being clear about **purpose**, **audience** and **register (PAR)** is an essential skill for doing Paper 1. It is particularly important when it comes to the personal essay question.

exam focus

Identify the **idea** or concept suggested in each personal essay title. If you don't know enough about the concept, don't do the essay.

key point

Check past exam papers and study the visuals, which usually accompany Comprehension Text 3. **Practise short paragraphs** inspired by these visuals.

Purpose

Ask yourself what your essay aims to achieve. If you intend to describe paradise, as one of the essay options of 2008 asked, your essay must be one that would genuinely appeal to any reader. It must be convincing. You will have to include the **language of persuasion**, along with some **narration** and **aesthetics.**

Audience

Consider who you are writing the essay for. Obviously the examiner will read your essay, but you should write with the presumption that it could be read and appreciated by others. Therefore, you should imagine that you are writing for someone you can trust. Think of your reader as someone who won't judge you, but is **interested in hearing you say something interesting**.

Register

Remember that register involves many elements. It requires: specific **vocabulary**, appropriate **tone**, and proper **treatment of the task** at hand.

It is helpful to fill out a **PAR plan** before you write a personal essay. Examine the plan for 'My Idea of Paradise' below.

My Idea of Paradise		
Purpose	**Audience**	**Register**
● To show that I have a clear idea of the concept: paradise. ● To describe clearly my version of paradise.	● Friends who would understand me. ● People who would not ridicule my view, but ask questions about it. ● The examiner, who will grade my effort.	● Sincere: it needs to sound like I really mean it. ● Light-hearted: since it is a pleasant topic. ● Convincing: I need to explain myself well and convince the examiner of my point of view.

Personal essay based on visuals (Pictures)

- If you decide to write a personal essay in response to the visuals on your exam paper, be very sure about your choice. If you **like reading visual texts**, then a personal essay based on visuals might be the perfect choice for you. For a reminder of how to respond to visuals, look at Chapter 4, pp. 27–29 and follow the advice found there.

Clarity and Coherence

The Composition section is a tremendous test of your vocabulary and expression. There are many tips and language aids available for this question. However, the most important thing to remember is the need for **clarity and coherence**:

- Have **clear ideas** in your head. Think before you write!
- Write **coherent sentences**. This means keeping things simple and understandable.

You cannot go far wrong if you keep these things in mind.

Sentences

Below is some useful information about sentences:

- Each sentence must have a **subject**, i.e. something doing the action.
  Example: The **Shannon** is the longest river in Ireland.
- Each sentence must have a **verb**, i.e. the action word.
  Example: The Shannon **flows** through the midlands.
- Each sentence must be a **complete thought**.
- If one or more of these elements is missing, then you have a **phrase**, rather than a sentence.
  Examples: – flows through the midlands (no subject)
  – longest river in Ireland (no subject or verb)
- Using phrases rather than complete sentences can lead to lower quality writing. Always ensure your sentences contain: a subject, a verb and a complete thought.
- Sentences can become more complex, but if you **read** and **write** a lot you will gain confidence in structuring them.

Improving your expression

A **dictionary** or **thesaurus** can be very useful in improving your expression and adding depth to your sentences. Here is an example of a simple sentence:

The Shannon flows through the midlands.

This is a basic sentence using informative language. See how it changes when we add some **adjectives**. Adjectives are descriptive words used to modify nouns.

*The **majestic, sparkling** Shannon flows through the **lush, flat** midland region of Ireland.*

We can also include **adverbs**. Adverbs are descriptive words used to modify verbs.

*The majestic, sparking Shannon flows **lazily** through the lush, flat midland region of Ireland.*

We can even add new **phrases** or **clauses**.

*The majestic, sparkling Shannon, **Ireland's longest river**, flows lazily through the lush, flat midland region of the country.*

Notice how the extra clause is added; it is separated with commas. See how the end of the sentence is tweaked to avoid repetition. 'Region of Ireland' has become 'region of the country' to avoid repetition of the word 'Ireland'.

Paragraphs

A paragraph contains a series of sentences that are linked by the same theme or idea. Here are some tips on using paragraphs:

- Become comfortable with paragraphs by practising your essays regularly. All good compositions are paragraphed well.
- Start a new paragraph when you want to move to: a new point; a new location; a new idea; a new speaker; new dialogue; or when you want to conclude your essay.

- Paragraphs are strongly advised in exam answers because they show that you have put order and structure on your work.
- Even if you are not entirely certain, begin a new paragraph if you feel you should. Paragraphs always look better on the page than a big, solid block of text.

key point

Paragraphs are not optional!

Tips for avoiding some common pitfalls

- Aim for the *right* word, rather than a big word that you may not be able to use correctly.
- Regularly read a **thesaurus** to increase your vocabulary.
- Verbs, adjectives and adverbs should be varied as much as possible to breathe life and colour into your work.
- The composition might not actually be all about 'you', so try to avoid starting too many sentences with 'I' or having too many references to 'me'. Try thinking outside of yourself and try to see things from other points of view.
- Writing good **comedy** is considered very challenging because we all have a different sense of what we find funny. Seek advice from teachers or classmates beforehand. See if you have a gift for humorous writing. It might be a talent you can use in the exam.
- Stick to the task always. Answer the question asked. Be decisive and confident in your writing and don't write down that you 'don't know' things. Examiners want to reward what you know, not punish you for not knowing.

Meaningless words

'Verbiage' is a great word for what is also called waffle! This occurs when we include unnecessary words or when we use words that carry little or no meaning. Look at some examples below:

Smile *on his face*   (Where else would it be?)

Few *in number*   (Few already indicates a number.)

Past history   (History is in the past.)

Very unique   (Unique means one of a kind. There is no such thing as 'very unique'.)

Rectangular *shape* (A rectangle is a shape.)

Meet *together*   ('Meet' means coming together.)

Small *in size*   ('Small' indicates size.)

General public   (Is there a non-general public?)

If you read quality newspapers and books, you will avoid verbiage and you will understand and appreciate good writing.

Words and expressions to be avoided!

The following expressions do not exist:	The following expressions do exist, but they are used far too often!
• Could of • Would of • Might of • Should of • Alot	• Sort of • You know • Like

If you use coarse or vulgar language in your Leaving Certificate exam, your final grade will be seriously affected.

Emphatic words

When you use too many emphatic words, you imply that what you're saying is absolute fact and is not open to argument.

The following emphatic words should be used carefully:		
• Always	• None	• Absolute
• Never	• Total	• Entire
• All	• Complete	

Hyperbole

Hyperbole is pronounced 'hi-per-boh-lay' and means gross exaggeration. To describe Yeats as the 'greatest, most outstanding, supreme poet in any language whatsoever' might fit your beliefs, but it would be more measured to say: 'I admire Yeats for the following reasons ...'

Clichés

Try to avoid clichéd phrases. Use the table below to improve your writing. On the left are some particularly clichéd phrases. Think of original ways of expressing these same ideas and write your new phrases on the right.

A game of two halves	
Raining cats and dogs	
Daylight robbery	
Pure class	
Going forward	
In the current climate	
The writing is on the wall	

As black as coal	
As cold as ice	
As red as blood	
As blue as the sea	
As dark as night	
As white as snow	
At the end of the day	
Backs to the wall	
In this day and age	
Ordinary man in the street	
Leave no stone unturned	
Openness and transparency	
Cool, calm and collected	
To be sure	
A terrible tragedy	
Sight for sore eyes	
Knee high to a grasshopper	
Coming on leaps and bounds	

You might have to use clichés on occasion and the examiner might not penalise you too much for them. However, the whole idea of the exam is to test your expression. So think creatively and aim for originality!

6 The Single Text

- To outline key points to remember for Single Text revision.
- To identify the typical questions that could be asked in this section.
- To examine some texts in detail to show how to revise.

Getting started

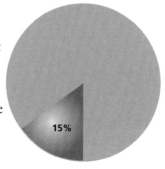

- You will have studied **ONE** text in detail for this part of the exam.
- The questions will be quite specific.
- The writing tasks are sometimes like those found in the comprehensions on Paper 1.
- There are 60 marks available – so spend around 55 minutes on this section.

15%

2020 Exam (Study ONE Text)

- ATWOOD, **Margaret** *The Handmaid's Tale*
- AUSTEN, **Jane** *Persuasion*
- BARRY, **Sebastian** *Days Without End*
- CARR, **Marina** *By the Bog of Cats*
- DONOGHUE, **Emma** *Room*
- ORWELL, **George** *1984*
- SYNGE, **J. M.** *The Playboy of the Western World*

2021 Exam (Study ONE Text)

- ATWOOD, **Margaret** *The Handmaid's Tale*
- BARRY, **Sebastian** *Days Without End*
- BRONTË, **Emily** *Wuthering Heights*
- CARR, **Marina** *By the Bog of Cats*
- DONOGHUE, **Emma** *Room*
- FRIEL, **Brian** *Philadelphia, Here I Come!*
- ORWELL, **George** *1984*

There are several questions/exam pages in Paper 2 that are of no relevance to you on the day. Identify your chosen 'Single Text' and ignore the others.

Revising the Single Text

There are nine 'Single Text' options each year and you must write answers on **ONE** of them.

You **cannot then use that same text again** in any other section. You will be severely penalised and lose a lot of marks if you do.

Ordinary Level students do **NOT** have to study Shakespeare – often, your teacher will choose one of the other seven texts instead.

> **key point**
>
> You must know the difference between the 'Single Text' and 'Comparative Texts' before the exam starts. Each school and teacher will make different choices.

Answering questions

When answering exam questions, your answers should follow a familiar format:

POINT – QUOTE – EXPLAIN OR 'P.Q.E.'

This means that you must **write something**, include supporting **quotes or references** and then follow things up with some **further explanation of your own**.

Examiners will be on the look-out for this approach to answers on Paper 2 especially.

Question format

60 marks in total

- **Three 10-mark questions – Do all three – 30 minutes**
- **Three longer 30-mark questions – Do ONE – 25 minutes**

10-mark questions

- Comment on **specific moments** or issues in the text.
- Comment on a **specific character** and their role in the text.
- Your answers should be **precise. Stick to what the question asks.** You should write six or seven full sentences and address the question directly with your opening sentence.

> **key point**
>
> You must use your time wisely so always remember the number of marks per question.

- Follow the **'statement–quotation–comment'** approach; i.e. say something to begin with, include a quote or reference, then finish with a follow-up comment.
- Spend a maximum of 10 minutes on each answer and no more than **30 minutes in total for these three questions.**
- If you are running out of time, **finish what you are doing and move on** – there are many more sections to come.

30-mark questions

Since there are **30 marks** available, spend no more than **25 minutes** on this question. This includes writing a **short plan or brainstorm before you begin.** These are the types of questions that you should **practice beforehand when studying.**

Typical tasks

- Take a **personal point of view** on a theme/issue in the studied text.
- Imagine that you are 'character x' and write an **account of a key moment.**
- **Write a journalistic article** of some sort based upon the events of the studied text.
- **Write a diary/journal entry** of a key character.
- **Write a letter** to/from a character from the text.

The writing skills needed on Paper 1 are just as important in Paper 2.

Selected Single Texts

You just need to revise **ONE** text.

We will concentrate our notes on **six of the more popular texts** suggested for Ordinary Level students.

We will focus on the three key elements of revision:

a) the storyline/plot

b) the characters

c) two main themes and issues

Find the notes below for your chosen text.

1. *The Handmaid's Tale* by Margaret Atwood (2020/21)

Important note on studying this text

Atwood's novel (1985) has been made into a film (1990) and more recently a TV series (2017 onwards). While these adaptations are interesting, the Leaving Cert requires you to study the novel only. It can be confusing if you decide to watch the film, and especially confusing if you watch the TV series. Ensure that you focus on revising the novel only when preparing for the exam in June.

Storyline

Published in 1985, Margaret Atwood set *The Handmaid's Tale* **sometime in the future**, roughly the early 21st century. It contains a number of interesting plot features, twists and unusual circumstances. Though brilliantly written and highly regarded, it can be a challenging book to read.

- The United States of America is now called **Gilead** and has changed hugely. The story is told by **the female protagonist, a Handmaid named Offred**, who recounts her daily life, sometimes through flashbacks and snippets. This allows the reader to **reconstruct the events** leading up to the beginning of the novel.

- Offred is not her real name (it is never fully revealed), instead she is known as Offred, with the suffix 'Fred' denoting her association with the **Commander**. Her name is a play-on-words or pun on the idea of being 'offered' up.

- Gilead is a **totalitarian state**, where freedom is strictly controlled, and where a **ruthless and severe form of Christianity** has replaced the previous system of democracy.

- People have been separated into strict categories with specific roles. Effectively, Gilead is a **white supremacist and Christian fundamentalist dystopian society**.

- Offred was originally married to **Luke** and she is the mother of a **five-year-old daughter**. She had attempted to escape to Canada, away from Gilead. She was caught and separated from her family.

- She has not seen Luke nor her daughter since, and frequently yearns to be with them again. Her own **mother** also disappeared at this time.

- Offred is selected as a potential 'breeder' or **Handmaid** and is given the **long red uniform and white head covering**. Other women wear different colours to indicate their position. **Marthas** are infertile women chosen to do domestic work. **Econowives** are poorer women, married to lower-ranked men and producing lower-classed babies.

- Offred is held and controlled at the '**Rachel and Leah Re-Education Centre**' **(RED Centre)** named after two women from the Old Testament. It's similar to a prison inside a compound, surrounded by fences topped by barbed wire. After training is complete here, Handmaids are selected to work for a Commander.

- She meets up with her old, rebellious college friend **Moira**, a lesbian, and they grudgingly follow the direction of the female bosses, the **Aunts**, particularly **Aunt Lydia** and **Aunt Elizabeth**.

- Everything Offred and Moira say or do is closely monitored, not just by the Aunts but also by their fellow Handmaids, creating **a climate of paranoia and fear**.

- The Handmaids offer each other **small secret comforts**, such as touching hands briefly at night time as they sleep beside each other.

- Moira eventually escapes but is captured soon after. She chooses to work as a prostitute in Jezebel's, a brothel set up for the needs of the Commanders, instead of facing certain death in the colonies beyond Gilead.

- Offred serves the Commander and his wife, **Serena Joy**, an advocate for traditional family values and a former Gospel singer.

- The door to Offred's room must always be open and the **Eyes**, Gilead's **secret police force**, watch her every move.

- Offred tells us of the **Ceremony** in which the Commander reads from the Bible, then goes to the bedroom, where his wife and Offred wait for him. He has sex with Offred as Serena sits behind her, holding her hands. This happens monthly **in the hopes of pregnancy**.

- However, one day, Offred visits the doctor and he offers to have sex with her to get her pregnant, suggesting that **her Commander is probably infertile**. She refuses, knowing how dangerous such a move would be. She truly trusts nobody.

- Offred is partnered with **Ofglen**, a rebellious Handmaid. They go to the shops together and on these trips, they develop a relationship.

- Ofglen tells Offred of a secret organisation named **Mayday**. The organisation seeks to overthrow Gilead and return the country to its former self. She hopes Offred can help with the secret plans of Mayday.

- After a while, Offred becomes somewhat attached to the Commander, but the relationship is uncertain and complicated. He tries to win her affections, offering her gifts and eventually letting her dress differently.

- They play Scrabble (which is forbidden, since women are not allowed to read) and he lets her look at magazines. Eventually, **he asks her to kiss him**.

- The Commander then takes Offred away to Jezebel's, full of Commanders and other powerful men from many nationalities. They engage in sex in an upstairs room.

- After Offred fails to conceive during the monthly Ceremony ritual, Serena suggests that Offred have sex with **Nick**, who is employed by the Commander as a gardener, driver and low-ranking officer in Gilead. They must then pretend that the Commander is the father.

- This is a central moment in the story: **it could make or break Offred's future**. In return, Serena promises to bring Offred a picture of her daughter.

- Offred realises that **Serena has always known the whereabouts of her daughter**. Shortly after this, Offred begins visiting Nick regularly.

- Offred becomes caught up in this affair and **ignores Ofglen's earlier request** that she gathers information from the Commander for Mayday. She starts to feel close to Nick.

- Sometime later, all the Handmaids take part in a **group execution** of a supposed rapist, supervised by Aunt Lydia. Ofglen strikes the first blow. Later, she tells

Offred that the so-called rapist was **a member of Mayday** and that she hit him to ensure he would not suffer a worse fate.

- Shortly thereafter, a new Ofglen meets Offred. This new woman is not part of Mayday, and she tells Offred that **the old Ofglen hanged herself** when she saw the secret police coming for her.

- At home, **Serena has found out about Offred's trip to Jezebel's** and she sends her to her room, promising punishment. Offred waits there and she sees a black van from the Eyes approach.

- Then Nick comes in and tells her that **the Eyes are really Mayday members** who have come to save her. Offred leaves with them, on her way either to prison or to freedom, **we never find out which it is**.

Epilogue

The novel closes with an **epilogue from 2195 A.D.**, after Gilead has been overthrown. It is written as a lecture given by a **Professor Pieixoto**. He discusses the importance of Offred's story, which has turned up on cassette tapes in Bangor, Maine. He suggests that Nick arranged Offred's escape but that **her fate after that is unknown**. She could have escaped to Canada or England, or she could have been recaptured. This is how the novel ends.

Five Key Words

- **Handmaid** – a fertile woman, required to produce children in Gilead
- **Commander** – a powerful, elite man who is required to impregnate a Handmaid
- **Ceremony** – the ritual of sexual intercourse in Gilead
- **Mayday** – a secret resistance group, trying to topple Gilead
- **Prayvaganza** – public religious events, designed to brainwash and control

CHARACTERS

1) Offred

- Offred never reveals her real name but from the opening pages, it is possible that she was originally named June. She has no family or friends to speak of, though she has flashbacks to a time in which she had a daughter and a husband named Luke. **The cruelty of her daily life in Gilead torments her** and in effect, this account of life is true not just for the Handmaids, but for all inhabitants of Gilead.

- By choosing not to name her, Atwood emphasises how **Offred's identity is entirely erased** and replaced with one completely dependent on her Commander. This is also tied to Offred's role in Gilead, effectively as a breeding machine, and how it is used to ensure the powerful have offspring to follow in their footsteps.

- But Offred is also rebellious in her own mind. In Chapter 5, she reflects on the idea of freedom and makes an important distinction: '*There is more than one kind of freedom ... freedom to and freedom from.*' A Handmaid must give up so many free things in order to live. She is no longer free 'to' do things. But she is also free 'from' other troubling things like disease, illness, poverty and infertility. While not fully accepting her situation, she is determined to survive her circumstances, even risking execution by establishing a relationship with Nick and believing in a possible escape.

- We can **admire Offred's ability** to cope with the level of personal anxiety and paranoia in her world. She is able to tell of these awful times in very clear detail. On the other hand, a Handmaid named **Janine** has totally surrendered to the rulers of Gilead and **appears weak in the eyes of Offred**. Offred is attracted instead to the rebelliousness of both Moira and the first Ofglen, and remains keenly observant and aware of her situation to the end.

- Her **eye for detail**, her **vivid memories** and her **account of the vicious cruelty of Gilead** allows Atwood to paint a picture of a dystopian world through Offred's personal experience.

2) The Commander

- The Commander is the head of the household where Offred works as a Handmaid. He **controls their relationship** – although he may have less influence over his relationship with his wife Serena, who seems devious. **He attempts to appear decent**, a man who is prepared to put the ideology of Gilead in place, to impregnate a Handmaid and safeguard the nation, to do 'his duty' as befits his rank. But in another way, he could be considered a serial rapist, having monthly sex with a woman placed in this position against her will, her only other option being an almost certain death.

- Another difficulty with his character is that he may be an **unintended victim of Gilead totalitarianism**. He attempts to share some tender moments with Offred, such as playing Scrabble and providing her with various clothes to wear. He appears to seek a genuine intimacy of sorts. Offred sometimes finds that she likes him in spite of everything. Secretly, **he might be making the best of a society he actually opposes**. Like much of the book, his true thoughts are not made explicitly clear, nor can we totally trust what he says.

- However, we learn from various clues in the text and from the epilogue that the Commander was actually involved in creating Gilead. To consider him as some sort of victim is to ignore the **dystopian and dysfunctional world he participates quite enthusiastically in**.

3) Serena Joy

- As the Commander's infertile wife, **Serena Joy is neither of the two things that her name may suggest**. This is actually her stage name, when in pre-Gilead days she was a Gospel singer, then a vocal 'anti-feminist' activist who worked passionately for 'traditional values'. We have no idea what her actual name is, other than 'the Commander's Wife.'

- She is **desperately unhappy** and serves very little function in Gilead now, other than to partake in the sex ceremony. It is Offred who makes the most telling observation: *'Which of us is it worse for, her or me?'*

- Serena initially encourages Offred to break the law to try for pregnancy, but when she hears of other sins on Offred's part, we see that **jealousy and bitterness are not far from the surface**. Serena's unhappiness shows that this male-dominated society cannot bring happiness even to its most pampered, powerful and wealthy women.

4) Moira

- A long-time friend of the narrator, **Moira, is a rebel at heart** who is **tenacious** and stands up for herself. They have known each other since college and Moira is the **only direct living link Offred has with the previous world**. (We cannot be sure about Luke or other family members.) She demands her own rights and represents the typical reaction of the marginalised or the downtrodden, at least initially. She did manage to escape the Red Centre breaking a toilet to do so.

- **She just won't forget about the 'time before'** and the world that used to be. She is an inspiration, even if secretly, to those other women and Handmaids who dream of real freedom one day.

- **Moira's ultimate fate** however, like many of the other characters, **remains unresolved**. When we last hear about her, she is working at Jezebel's and her spirit seems broken. The fact that she would rather accept work as a prostitute in Jezebel's than head to the colonies demonstrates that Gilead has simply worn her down. Her eventual fate remains undisclosed and she is **ultimately a sad figure in this story**.

5) Aunt Lydia

- Aunt Lydia works at the Red Centre, the re-education centre where Offred and other women go for instruction before becoming Handmaids. She says what is perhaps the most frightening of all the quotes in the book, in Chapter 6: *'This may not be ordinary to you now, but after a time it will. This will become ordinary.'*

- What makes this statement so terrifying is that the novel strongly suggests that **Aunt Lydia is right**. If people continue to do their duties as ordered, eventually, if enough time passes, they may forget what it was like to live in a free, democratic world. **'Normal' becomes whatever the rulers of such a world demand.** She appears only in Offred's flashbacks and her words haunt her daily life, drumming this new ideology into her head. For all these Handmaids, this ideology is almost impossible to ignore, feeding a kind of terror and emotional torment that won't relent. **In powerful tones, Aunt Lydia voices the propaganda of Gilead.**

6) Nick

- A good question to ask is whether Nick can be trusted at all. His final words to Offred, as she is bundled into the black van, implore that she should **'trust' him**. We must believe, therefore, that he is not an Eye but in fact part of the Mayday resistance movement. Nick is a **mysterious figure**, although unlike Luke, he exists in the narrator's present instead of just in her memory. Is he really just a gardener, a chauffeur, a handyman, a **handsome idiot?** Or is there more to him? From the beginning, the narrator considers him to be a suspicious character: *'He's too casual, he's not servile enough. It may be stupidity, but I don't think so.'* Offred is generally quite observant and hesitant so when she says *'I smell a rat'*, she may indeed be correct.

- By the later stages of the novel, Offred is desperate to pour out her feelings to Nick and it might well be that he is just a **lucky guy who takes advantage of a desperate woman**. His interest in Offred is most likely just sexual and in that light, his apparent passion for her can be seen for what it actually is – nothing more than lust and excitement in a highly-controlled world.

Other Characters

- **Luke** is Offred's former lover with whom she had a child. He is a constant memory evoked throughout, a symbol of future happiness. He had an affair with Offred while he was married to another woman, then got a divorce and became Offred's husband. He is separated from Offred and the couple never see one another again. Offred's memories of Luke contrasts with the passionless, regulated relations in the new society.

- **Ofglen** is another Handmaid, Offred's shopping partner and a member of Mayday. At the end of the novel, Ofglen is found out and she hangs herself rather than face torture and reveal the names of her co-conspirators.

- **Cora** works as a servant in the Commander's household. She is a **Martha**, an infertile woman who does not qualify for high status and instead carries out domestic work. Cora seems more content with her role than her fellow Martha, Rita. She hopes that Offred will be able to conceive because then she will have a hand in raising a child.

- The **Handmaid Janine** is always ready to go along with what Gilead demands of her, submitting to authority. Offred despises Janine for taking the easy way out and accepting this horrible fate.

Themes

1) Power

While there are numerous themes and issues in this novel, the most important theme by far is **power**, especially **the manipulation and abuse of power**. Almost all the major issues, characters and events bring the reader back to questions of power, control and freedom in one way or another.

Here are four possible areas to consider when revising:

- Atwood shows us a world in which **power is apparently held by men only. But this is not strictly true.** In order for this society to exist, there must be many people, including women, prepared to protect this power structure. The Aunts, in particular, encourage the sexual control held over women. Not to mention women like Serena Joy, a former champion of 'family values', who initially accepts the Handmaids into the house and then proceeds to treat them with utter contempt and disdain. To describe the theme of power in the novel as simply 'men-controlling-women' is not as accurate as detailing the layers within this power structure, **layers in which various women also safeguard the ideals of Gilead**.

- Another characteristic of **this kind of power is its extreme visibility**. Soldiers with guns are everywhere and a general sense of fear and paranoia is maintained among the public. Sinners are executed and their bodies are displayed publicly. The ideals of Gilead are always on show. Furthermore, by sending pairs of Handmaids shopping in clear daylight, Gilead presents their status, like all other women, as second rank to the rest of the community. This power structure is **designed to turn people, perhaps even close friends or associates, upon each other** if they deviate from the norm. It means nobody can really be trusted, not even the people you are closest to.

- A third characteristic of this type of power is the way in which individual **people still manage to find ways around its abuses**. The only place that people are really free in Gilead is in their own heads. This is an important message in the novel and is central to the journey of Offred through her various ordeals. She comes to realise that **her sexuality, no matter how restricted it is, is her only source of power in this dystopian world**. In understanding the importance of her fertility as a woman, Offred can successfully manipulate authority. She knows that she can create desire in men and build up an inevitable jealousy in other women. While it is dangerous for Offred to disobey the expected norms of a Handmaid's role, her awareness of her own power means that she can cope better than others with the challenges of being a Handmaid.

- Finally, one of the most memorable quotes of the novel is the Latin phrase that Offred discovers scraped in her room by a previous inmate: *'Nolite te bastardes carborundorum'*. It roughly translates as **'Do not let the bastards grind you down'**. There is some reflection in the book as to who actually wrote it and much debate in the real world as to whether the phrase is an accurate translation or not. But the

message is quite clear and precise; it sums up the best response one can have to a structure in which power is being abused so noticeably.

exam Q

SAMPLE QUESTION AND ANSWER (30 MARKS/25 MINUTES)

The Handmaid's Tale by Margaret Atwood (2020/2021)

Question

Write a piece in which you compare how Offred and Moira cope with life in the Republic of Gilead. Support your answer with reference to the novel.

SAMPLE ANSWER

The kind of relationship that Moira and Offred have, since their college days, does not exist in Gilead anymore. The closest we get to a genuine friendship in *The Handmaid's Tale* is between these two female characters. The concept of friendship is one of the casualties of this new world – everybody is suspicious of everybody else. But I think Offred and Moira know each other in a much deeper way and manage to maintain friendship, at least as long as they are in contact with each other. However, they have very different ways of coping with the miseries they face.

I think Moira is the more interesting of the two when it comes to how she copes with Gilead's society. I would describe her as defiant, brave and heroic. She is a lesbian, meaning that she does not conform to the strict male–female sexual code of Gilead. She reminds us of a more liberal past, or in the eyes of Gilead, a sinful bygone era. But more than that, she is the only character who stands up to authority directly. She attempts to escape from the Red Centre twice, the second time successfully. And by stealing the clothes of the Aunt, she proves to us that she won't be bound by rules of dress, behaviour or the restriction of her individual freedom. It is easy to admire Moira but the fact that she ends up a prostitute in Jezebel's, servicing men, is a depressing end. The lesson from the book is that even the most rebellious of people like Moira can be completely crushed by a regime as cruel as Gilead.

If Moira is the rebel and the other Handmaid Janine is completely submissive to the tyranny of Gilead, then Offred falls somewhere in the middle. She tries to blend in as best as she can – this is a way of coping with trauma.

Offred is intelligent, perceptive and kind-hearted. It makes her a good narrator of the novel but at the same time, she is not exactly a hero or a champion that we should admire. She copes with Gilead by managing to conceal her true feelings and thoughts, while outwardly trying to fit in with Gilead's rules. I think she becomes more passive and acceptant of Gilead as things unfold. Life become almost normal. It is really Nick who arranges her escape rather than any attempt made by herself.

Also, Offred frequently presents us with flashbacks of her previous life – her memories of Luke, their child, happier times back in college, among other things. This is another coping mechanism, thinking of pleasant times past and retaining hope that one day that version of the world might return. Given the way the novel ends, as she is bundled into the black van, we cannot be sure if it works out for her at all.

In the end, Offred and Moira are two of the many ordinary women of this dystopian world who try their best to cope with an extraordinary situation. They both have their own way of coping; Moira is outwardly rebellious and Offred is more reflective and passive.

(522 words)

EXAMINER'S ASSESSMENT

Lots of detail here and the candidate is familiar with the characters and the plot. The language is of a very good standard and the answer is structured. However, it lacks quotation or more detailed referenced in order to achieve the top marks. Point-Quote-Explain would improve the grade.

MARKS AWARDED

7 + 7 + 7 + 3 = 24/30 (O2 Grade)

2. *1984* by George Orwell (2020/21)

Storyline

George Orwell wrote this remarkable novel just after the end of World War II. It is set in a future London that is nothing like the city today; it is a **dystopian** world, one where things have gone badly wrong for its citizens. This novel is probably the most famous and celebrated dystopian novel ever written.

- **Oceania** is the new name for the state and it is constantly at war with two other states: Eurasia and Eastasia.

- Oceania is governed by the all-controlling **Party**, which has bullied and brainwashed the population into obeying its leader, the mysterious **Big Brother**.

- This is what is known as a **totalitarian** regime; a society in which individual freedom of any sort is banned.

- The book's supposed hero is **Winston Smith**. He is a low-ranking worker for the Party, whose job involves rewriting history in the **Ministry of Truth**, to brainwash the population and remove all individual thought and ideas.

- The Party has slogans such as **'War is peace'**, **'Freedom is slavery'**, and **'Ignorance is strength'**, all examples of what the Party calls **Doublespeak**, i.e. the ability to say and believe whatever you are told to say and believe.

- They control people's actions through the **Thought Police**. Television screens and advertisements constantly display the words: **'BIG BROTHER IS WATCHING YOU'**.

- Winston's decency and bravery leads him to rebel against the government. He commits two crimes: he **purchases a diary** in which to write his criminal thoughts and he begins a **forbidden affair with Julia**, a beautiful, like-minded co-worker, who passes him a note saying 'I Love You'.

- This secret but genuine relationship lasts for some time, despite **constant surveillance** and the threat of capture.

- They hear of a mysterious **Brotherhood**, a revolutionary group bound to overthrow the Party. They suspect that a high-ranking Party official named **O'Brien** may actually be an undercover member of the Brotherhood. Winston agrees to meet him one day.

- This turns out to be a trap. **Mr Charrington**, the man who sold Winston the diary and who also facilitated the love affair with Julia, is actually a member of the Thought Police.

- Winston and Julia are arrested and sent to the **Ministry of Love** for a violent brainwashing (or re-education), and the relationship is ended.
- The subsequent **torture of Winston** is brutal and shocking, aimed at breaking him physically and destroying his dignity, humanity and independent thought all at once.
- Following numerous sessions in **Room 101**, Winston finally loses his sanity as a cage of rats is attached to his head. He yells out for his tormentors to '*Do it to Julia!*' and states that he does not care what happens to her.
- With this betrayal, Winston is released. He now even believes that '**2+2=5**' demonstrating the extent of the damage done.
- He later encounters Julia but neither is interested in the other. Giving up Julia is what O'Brien wanted from Winston all along.
- His spirit broken, Winston has become what the Party demanded. '**Winston now loved Big Brother**', the final words of the novel declare.

Five Key Words

- **Oceania** – the new name for the civilised world run by the Party
- **Proles** – Oceania population that are not Party members, living in poverty
- **Newspeak** – the official language of Oceania
- **Thoughtcrime** – doubting Big Brother or questioning any Party action
- **Doublethink** – words or ideas, spoken together, that contradict each other

CHARACTERS

1) Big Brother

- At no stage in the novel do we meet an actual man with this name. Instead, Big Brother is the **figurehead or symbol** of the Party, a middle-aged man with a bristly moustache, depicted on posters and other official materials. His presence in the novel is as a looming figure, **representing the desired 'thinking' or ideas of the Party**. Supporters of the Party enjoy seeing Big Brother as a protective old uncle or a Santa Claus figure always 'watching you.' But people like Winston also see him as an ominous, threatening figure who frightens people into line.
- What is so brilliant about the Big Brother character is that he is **no more than an idea or concept**; those who invented him can use his powerful image to justify any and all commands that come from them. He **symbolises the abuse of power and control of freedom** that many totalitarian governments use, even today, to spread fear and paranoia among the wider population.

2) Winston Smith

- Winston is the **protagonist** of the novel. His actions at first appear heroic, yet he ultimately **fails to defeat the evil he faces**. He undergoes enormous personal suffering and by the end of the story, he becomes exactly the sort of person he was trying to avoid becoming.

- Outwardly, Winston Smith is a **shy, obedient and fairly unremarkable** member of the Party. Aged 39, he remembers the past, before the catastrophic war, and supports the Party only out of fear and necessity. Physically, **he looks older than he is**, as he moves stiffly with a bent back. He is in poor health overall, though without any specific disease. This represents the **repression and psychological torment** of being controlled by an outside force such as the Party.

- Despite this, he has an **idealism** about him that wants to see the world changed. We see how he practises his facial expressions and how he is always on high alert, even in his apartment. This is all part of his preparation for rebellion.

- He is motivated by **restlessness and a sense of dignity**. A happy, romantic ending would see him walk off with Julia into married life. Unfortunately, **he never truly believes** that he will succeed in his rebelliousness. As soon as he writes '**DOWN WITH BIG BROTHER**' in his diary, Winston is positive that the **Thought Police** will quickly capture him for committing a thoughtcrime. He also **takes numerous risks**, such as trusting O'Brien and renting the room above Mr Charrington's shop. Deep down, he knows that he will eventually be caught out, yet he convinces himself that he must continue to rebel. **It is this idealism and determination which ironically makes him suitable for the Party's agenda.** He concludes with the observation that it had taken 40 years to see the real truth: **he loved Big Brother after all**.

3) Julia

- Julia works at the Ministry of Truth, stationed (ironically enough) at the **Anti-Sex League**. She is **beautiful**. Like Winston, **she secretly despises the Party** but outwardly behaves obediently, as a member should. Julia's rebellion is centred not on political revolution or changing the world, but on personal desires. Her **sexuality is a source of empowerment**. She seeks out personal satisfaction in her own private and intimate way – most especially in loving Winston. Julia pretends to be a revolutionary: she follows with Winston's plans to be part of the Brotherhood. While she has **little real interest in their goals**, she goes along with it because it creates excitement in her life and ultimately, it is the **only real avenue for freedom in the long run**. Things unravel very badly for her, following capture. By the end of the novel, **Julia is physically and emotionally destroyed**. She dislikes Winston and leaves the Ministry of Love a shell of her former self.

4) O'Brien

- The novel has a lingering **sense of mystery and distrust**, particularly around the activities within the Party. **This uncertainty is represented best in the character of O'Brien**. He is Winston's boss at the Ministry and a high-ranking member of the Party. But Winston suspects that O'Brien sympathises with the Resistance and becomes excited when **he discovers (falsely) that O'Brien is a member of the Brotherhood**. O'Brien later appears and contributes to Winston's torture.

- O'Brien is a character that students must see as being completely false and unreliable. Most of what we learn about him is later revealed to be inaccurate. **We actually know nothing reliable about O'Brien at all**, other than the fact that he works for the Party. This makes him strongly representative of the dystopia that Orwell creates, a world where everything is potentially a lie. It builds the foundation on which people can be easily manipulated and abused according to the will of the Party. What is also fascinating is that **we do not really know the motivations of O'Brien nor do we know much of his backstory**. When asked about it by Winston, he merely states: '*They got me long ago.*' As to whether he was once like Winston, if there exists an actual Big Brother, or even a Resistance, these questions all remain unanswered. **O'Brien symbolises this shadowy world where nothing and nobody can be trusted.**

5) Mr Charrington

- Another character who is revealed to be something other than what we first suspect is Mr Charrington. He **seems to be a kind, old man**, aged about 60, who rents Winston a private room and sells him some interesting antiques. Winston believes that Mr Charrington may have once been a writer or musician and notes that he speaks with an accent '**less debased than that of the majority of proles**' (the proles being the ordinary working people of the novel). He has an interest in history which Winston shares. He **provides Winston with the opportunity and means to commit various crimes against the Party**.

- Mr Charrington sells Winston both the blank book which Winston uses to record a diary and also the glass paperweight, a symbol of Winston's memory of past times. The room is also the venue for some of Winston and Julia's sexual encounters. However, it is little surprise to the reader that Charrington is a member of the Thought Police and he has **been setting Winston up for arrest** all along. He is deeply involved in the deception that the Party engages in. It shows that Winston and Julia's fates are **controlled from the very beginning**.

6) Syme

- **Friendship** is a very rare commodity in Oceania. Syme is the **nearest that Winston has to a friend**, although he annoys him occasionally. He enjoys having some interesting conversations with him as **Syme specialises in language**. As the novel opens, he is working on the eleventh edition of the **Newspeak Dictionary** for the Records Department. Winston notices that Syme, although a devoted Party member, is **perhaps too intelligent for his own good**. He predicts Syme will be killed and is proven correct when he suddenly disappears.

Themes

1) Power and Control

More than any other theme (there are many in this novel), the **power and control that governments hold over their citizens** is essentially the main one to focus on.

- Orwell presents a **chilling version of a possible future** – a dystopia – where the absolute power of the Party has destroyed so much of what we value in a free democratic society: independent movement, thought, ideas, art, industry, enterprise and sexual expression between consenting adults.

- **Orwell was deeply disturbed by the widespread cruelty** he observed, particularly in communist countries, in the 1940s. He also seems to have been concerned by **the role of technology** in enabling such **totalitarian** governments to monitor and control their citizens. Hence, the novel is full of interesting descriptions of futuristic gadgets, machines and techniques used to communicate with, and control, both the **actions** and the **minds** of the people.

- The **physical control** of people is initially seen in the Party forcing its members to undergo morning exercises called the **Physical Jerks**, and then to work very long days at government agencies, keeping people in a general state of exhaustion. Anyone who does manage to defy the Party is punished and **'re-educated'** through brutal torture techniques. After being subjected to it himself, Winston comes to the conclusion that *'nothing is more powerful than physical pain'*. By conditioning the minds of their victims with physical torture, the Party is therefore able to control reality, convincing its subjects that '2 + 2 = 5'.

- Controlling people's minds, or **psychological control**, is seen through the constant stream of propaganda on wall-to-wall telescreens and loudspeakers. Everywhere they go, citizens are continuously reminded that **'BIG BROTHER IS WATCHING YOU'**, that they are being constantly scrutinised. Children are forced into an organisation called the **Junior Spies**, encouraging them to spy on their parents and report any disloyalty to the Party.

- **Suppressing sexual desires** and presenting the act of sex as merely a means for procreation creates an atmosphere of huge frustration and emotional turmoil. This emotion is transformed into vicious displays of hatred against any enemy of the

Party. Many of these enemies – such as **Emmanuel Goldstein** – have probably been invented by the Party for this purpose.

- Therefore, since **the Party controls the means and source of all information and communication**, they are able to manipulate the people, both physically and psychologically. It allows them to control both the past and the present world, **creating a truly chilling, disturbing view of the future**. And any individual, such as Winston Smith, who has other ideas will be dealt with in a brutal manner.

2) Identity

- Both Winston and Julia represent a common desire in all people as they journey through life: they both ask themselves **'Who am I?' and 'What is my purpose in this life?' and 'How can I be happy?'** What the novel teaches them – as well as its readers – is that the individual is essentially 'nobody' in this dystopian world. Who you are, what you should do and how to be happy are all determined by the Party.

- The Party, therefore, destroys all sense of independence and individuality. Everyone wears the same clothes, eats the same food and lives the same regulated, organised lives. No-one is allowed to 'stand out', nobody can be unique. To have an independent thought can lead to severe persecution. People are only permitted to think what the Party tells them to think, and do what the Party allows them to do. Therefore, **all sense of individual identity is wiped away** in Oceania.

- Both Winston and Julia's downfall occurs because they **believe that they are special** individuals who can stand out. Winston, in writing his diary, and Julia in passing a note and having love affairs, initially think this individualist streak will bring about change. But the torture they endure and the conclusions they share demonstrates the futility of trying to forge unique identities for themselves.

- The Party also recognises that **identity can be manipulated to suit a political agenda**. It is impossible to know for sure if the Brotherhood and its leader, Emmanuel Goldstein, actually exist. Similarly, we cannot know if there is an actual **Big Brother**, an individual or even an organised group that rules Oceania. By erasing personal identity and creating a cloud over who is actually in control, the conditions for the widespread abuse, control and torture of citizens are put in place.

exam focus

Look carefully at how the writing skills in Paper 1 are then applied to 30-mark questions in Paper 2. Look at the example on the next page.

SAMPLE QUESTION AND ANSWER (30 MARKS/25 MINUTES)

1984 by George Orwell (2020/2021)

Question

How are women portrayed in the novel *1984*? In your answer, refer to **TWO** women who play a significant role in the story.

SAMPLE ANSWER

The women in *1984* are stereotyped as mostly weak and useless. None of them are heroic or enjoyable to read about. Their main function seems to be as tools for reproduction and as facilitators for male sexual desire. They obediently follow the orders of the Party. However, Julia appears to be a little different to this, at least at the start. She is the dark-haired girl that Winston had admitted having a sexual attraction towards. She is indeed very beautiful and is working for the Anti-Sex League, which I found rather ironic. She secretly despises the Party but outwardly behaves obediently as a member of the Party should. She wears the red sash of chastity to confirm her role.

What makes her interesting is that she is the rebel in a world of conformity. Initially, Winston hates her. Like all such women: *'He hated her because she was young and pretty and sexless, because he wanted to go to bed with her and would never do so.'* She appears as a source of frustration, irritation and temptation. But her note telling Winston that she 'loves him' changes him instantly. They develop their relationship but by the end of the novel, we see that her rebellion was all quite false. Julia actually just pretended to be a revolutionary and she goes along with the plan to be part of the Brotherhood. But she has little real interest in their goals. She only went along because it created a sense of excitement in a very restricted life. So in the end, she was quite a disappointing character. Winston managed to sum her up well by saying that she is *'only a rebel from the waist downwards'*.

Winston's wife Katherine is another character that I initially found interesting but ultimately, she is described as being quite disappointing. When he first mentions her, Winston said: *'I could have endured living with her if it had not been for just one thing – sex'*. It indirectly points out that Winston agreed to have a wife just for the sake of his own sexual desire. He was living in a world where love and being loved in a genuine way was just impossible. The pleasure of sexual acts was banished, making it quite an unhappy place for both men and women. Katherine had also mentioned that making a baby was *'our duty to the Party'*, rather than something that a married couple would naturally do.

Overall, the fact that women are, for the most part, irrelevant in this dystopia shows how much of a disaster this world will be. Sexual and emotional frustration, for both men and women, only worsens the state of this society. Maybe a lot of the anger and aggression in this world is a result of the fact that men and women do not have what we would now call 'normal' relationships, even when married. Orwell really does emphasise how bad things can be if we don't fully respect women.

(532 words)

EXAMINER'S ASSESSMENT

A good attempt; covers two female characters and includes some quotation. A lot of emphasis on the sexuality aspect of the female characters; perhaps there are other insights (Julia is also daring, deceitful, self-interested, for example) so this answer falls short of top marks.

MARKS AWARDED

7 + 7 + 7 + 3 = 24/30 (O2 Grade)

3. *By the Bog of Cats* by Marina Carr (2020/21)

Storyline

The play is set in a **remote and desolate part of the Midlands of Ireland** known as 'the Bog of Cats'. It is a **'bleak white landscape of ice and snow'** at the beginning so we assume it is winter. The action unfolds in three acts: firstly, beside the house and caravan of Hester Swane, then in the home of Xavier Cassidy, then finally back again to the yard and the caravan of Hester.

- The entire play covers just one day in the life of this rural Irish community, beginning at dawn, taking in a local wedding that afternoon and finishing at nightfall with the death of a number of characters, most importantly Hester herself, the protagonist of the play.
- In this way, it mirrors a typical Greek tragedy. Specifically, **Hester is very similar to the Greek heroine Medea**, who herself was rejected by her husband and sought revenge.
- Hester is a **traveller woman**, born and reared on the Bog of Cats. She is an outsider in the community, despite having a child named **Josie**, fathered by

Carthage Kilbride, a local man from the settled community, and loving him for the last 14 years.

- The play opens with Hester speaking with a mysterious **Ghost Fancier** who observes that Hester has found the body of a dead black swan. It is the first of many omens that foreshadow the tragic events to come.

- Carthage is to marry Caroline Cassidy that afternoon and with the marriage, he will acquire the house that Hester currently occupies with Josie.

- Caroline arrives, dressed for her wedding, to confront Hester over the house but is no match for Hester's fierce defiance and pride. She tells her that '*Carthage Kilbride is mine and mine only*' and sends her on her way.

- Carthage arrives and Hester begs him to stay with her, reminding him of their long-standing relationship: '*Ya think you can wipe out fourteen years just like that.*' Carthage is not for turning, saying that the house and farm will be signed over to him after the wedding later that day.

- Caroline later returns with her father Xavier, who reminds Hester of how he cared for Hester as a child, given that her mother, **Big Josie Swane**, neglected her badly. This discussion paints a picture of Hester's very troubled and violent childhood.

- Xavier attempts to pay her off but Hester won't budge: '*I was born on the Bog of Cats and on the Bog of Cats I'll end my days.*' Like a number of things spoken in the play, it foreshadows tragic events. Hester also says that she liked her dead mother '*more than anything in this cold white world*'.

- At the wedding reception later that day, the **Catwoman** speaks to the ghost of **Joseph Swane**, Hester's dead brother. He needs to find Hester.

- The wedding is conducted by **Father Willow**, an incompetent and foolish priest, who makes little or no sense in his incoherent mumbling.

- Both **Xavier Cassidy**, father of the bride, and **Mrs Kilbride**, mother of the groom, deliver speeches that are both comical and pathetic, particularly Mrs Kilbride. She is jealous of Caroline and slightly traumatised from losing her son.

- Amidst the chaos, Hester arrives in her own wedding dress, to which Mrs Kilbride shouts: '*Ya piebald knacker ya!*' Hester begs Carthage to take her back, creating both panic and high amusement in the room. When he refuses, Hester then begs that she be left to live on the Bog, claiming that '*I can't go till me mother comes*'. Carthage absolutely refuses, meaning that Hester has no choice but to wage '*a vicious war against ya*'.

- That night, the ghost of Joseph Swane meets Hester as she burns down the house and sheds with cattle inside.

- We discover a terrible secret: **Hester murdered her brother years ago, jealous of him because her mother seemed to love him more.** They reconcile with each other, which prepares Hester for her own death.

- However, she is interrupted by the arrival of Carthage, Caroline and her own daughter Josie, who clings to her desperately: *'I'd be hopin' and waitin' and prayin' for ya to return.'*

- Caroline promises to take care of Josie, but in one last brutal, defiant act, Hester slits Josie's throat so that she will not endure the same fate as herself.

- She then meets the Ghost Fancier from the start of the play and they perform a 'dance of death' whereby Hester is stabbed in the heart and dies, killed by her own hand.

Five Key Words

- **Foreshadowing** – where future events are hinted at or suggested early on
- **Notions** – ideas of superiority that some people carry
- **Wagon** – a woman of questionable character
- **Knacker** – a derogatory term for an Irish Traveller
- **Not the full shilling** – suggesting that a person lacks their full mental capability

CHARACTERS

1) Hester Swane

- Everything that happens in this play **brings us back to Hester** in one way or another. As a traveller, she is an 'outsider' despite her long-existing relationship with Carthage Kilbride. Throughout, she is depicted as **strong-willed, proud, quick-witted, determined** and a match for anybody who crosses her. Her relationship with Carthage and the child they produced is a **discomfort for the villagers**, not least Carthage himself, who has now abandoned her for the younger Caroline. The play tells the story of how this **deeply passionate and sensitive woman**, a native of the Bog itself, deals with both her deep-rooted personal issues as well as the people around her who would gladly see her out of their lives forever.

- She is **proud of her heritage**, despite the very troubled past that lingers. Her conversation with the equally rejected and blind Catwoman (Act 1, Scene 3) is among the most important in the play. Despite being abandoned by her alcoholic and violent mother at a young age, she still has *'a longin' in me for her that won't quell the whole time'*. She expresses the universal longing for love and acceptance that all children have.

- The more we discover about her, the more we see her as **a victim of other people's neglect, greed, lust and rejection**. This is especially apparent in any of Hester's exchanges with Catwoman, her friend Monica and her daughter Josie. She is a tragic heroine even though she killed her brother and then her own daughter at the end of the play; she saves Josie from the same fate that befell her, ensuring that she won't feel neglected and abused the way she was. She reconciles with her brother before taking her own life, **an act considered noble in the tradition of tragedy**.

2) Carthage Kilbride

- His betrayal of Hester means that **Carthage is, on the surface, the villain of the play**. However, the bond between him and Hester had been genuine and the love they shared was real. His rejection of Hester in favour of Caroline represents a tendency to prefer the familiar and the 'safe', but also in this case, the promise of wealth and security. **Hester's way of life is one of survival**, determination and a close connection to the natural world and the ways of the past. With it comes much hardship, as evidenced in the story of both Hester and her mother Josie, as well as Catwoman. Carthage no longer wants this and **prefers the better social status and security that a marriage to Caroline brings**. He is also living under the influence of his mother, who seems to cause him embarrassment, especially at the wedding. By not managing to save his daughter Josie, **he is a failure as a father**, even if he finishes the play with the woman he wants for the future.

3) Mrs Kilbride

- Excessively **vain, self-absorbed and deluded**, Elsie Kilbride is more of a comic character than a villain, mostly because of how **stupidly arrogant** she sounds. She sees wealth and social status as the only proper measure of a person, hence her utter disdain for Hester and her silly taunting of her grand-daughter Josie. She is horrified that through Carthage, **she is tied to traveller blood forever**. To compensate, she insists on making a speech at her son's wedding to prove his love for her. She is a **shallow** and simple character to understand – one more to laugh at than to have any pity for.

4) Josie Kilbride

- Seven-year-old Josie demonstrates a **greater depth of character than her grandmother** and it is impossible not to admire her attention-seeking playfulness. She has had a relatively happy childhood and is free-spirited, with her 'tinker blood' and growing up on the bog. She does not want to lose the affections of her mother, pleading not to be left behind in the final scene. **There is an inevitability about her death**, as **foreshadowed** earlier in the play. To break the cycle of rejection and suffering, her mother kills her as an act of mercy, something quite shocking when seen onstage.

5) Caroline Cassidy

- She acts as a **contrast to Hester**, being very much the opposite to her: **young, innocent, well-loved, protected, optimistic and quite naive**. She has had a comfortable upbringing, despite losing her mother at a young age. Even though she lacks life experience, she does have enough insight to **recognise that a bond remains between Hester and Carthage**. She is brave enough to confront Hester at the start and is caring enough to promise to look after Josie near the end. She even admits to Hester that she didn't actually enjoy her wedding day. She sadly observes in Act 3 that *'none of it was how it was meant to be, none of it'*. It sums up her passive role in the play, whereby she has little or no control over the events unfolding.

6) Xavier Cassidy

- He **represents the typical country farmer**, wishing to see his only beloved daughter married off to a respectable young man. Having land and money affords him a lot of power and influence in this community, perhaps more than he deserves. Demanding to have the wedding reception in his house is a sign of this. There is a **particularly nasty streak** to him too. In Act 3, he confronts Hester in a sexually aggressive way, threatening to rape or perhaps kill her. There are also suggestions that he caused Big Josie Swane to leave Hester years ago, having taken advantage of her vulnerable situation. Beneath his outward show of respectability, **Xavier is a vile individual and more villainous than we are first led to believe**.

Other Characters

- **Catwoman** is an intriguing character, a witch-like individual who can see spirits and offer blessings, such as at the wedding. The locals both detest and admire her – she is physically quite disgusting but her blindness allows her see things more clearly than others. She *'knows everything that happens on this bog'* and despite trying to help Hester escape, she is unsuccessful.
- **Monica** is a neighbour who cares for Hester and Josie and is a **direct link to the past with Big Josie**, who she remembers well. Despite their differences, she is on Hester's side and tries to calm her rage in the final act.
- The ghostly figures of **Joseph** and the **Ghost Fancier** provide a contrast to the utterly useless **Father Willow**. This highlights the uselessness of organised religion to overcome the pagan, naturalistic forces that shroud the Bog of Cats.

Themes

1) The Outsider

The play emphasises the **plight of the outsider**, in this case, the traveller woman Hester Swane, and how she tries to **cope with harsh judgement**.

- The local community are constantly suspicious of her. For example, Mrs Kilbride does everything she can to get young Josie to disown her name, forcing her to spell the name Kilbride and regularly using the word 'ye' to describe her own grandchild and Josie's mother.

- Her insulting cry of '*ya piebald knacker*' at the wedding is the high-point of this type of racist language that can be found throughout the text.

- The relationship between Hester and Carthage only adds to the sense of discomfort here – the idea that settled people just simply should not have relationships with travellers.

- But Hester's outsider status is not just due to being a traveller. **She also chooses to live on the edge of society**, preferring the caravan on the desolate bog to the house built for her. She befriends another outsider, Catwoman, and has a quick-witted answer to anybody who speaks to her.

- Nothing is more important than the love and connection she has with her mother, her daughter and the land that they all were born into.

- **She is tormented by a terrible deed from the past** and wants for nothing more than to be reunited with her mother and dead brother. This personal plight, and the upheaval that the wedding brings, further complicates her outsider status.

- Hester also represents much of what a modern, **settled community would prefer to see left behind**, such as a nomadic way of life that is close to the natural world and pagan traditions.

- Hester is an **exceptionally strong and honest woman**, who sees beyond the deception and falseness of the locals, such as Mrs Kilbride and Xavier Cassidy. She speaks a truth that the settled community do not want to face up to:

  > '*As for me tinker blood: I'm proud of it. It gives me an edge over all of yees around here, allows me to see yees for the inbred, underbred, bog-brained shower yees are.*'

- The outsider Hester Swane has a fierce pride, determination and sense of identity that is unmatched by any of the locals. It is what makes the outsider the heroine of the play.

Symbolism

One of the most notable features of this play is that it is **heavily symbolic**. Names, places, characters, and the action itself can be seen to represent something deeper or hidden, like the way a bog preserves secret treasures from the past. Some interesting examples of symbolism include:

- **The bog** – a place where the past can literally be preserved. The storyline is centred around events from the past which come to haunt the present, much like discovering something ancient buried in the boggy ground.
- **Character names** – Hester is similar to Esther, a brave woman who risked her life to save her people; Swane is similar to 'swain' or 'young, rustic male' – Hester is fiercely aggressive, more like the temperament of a young man; the Kilbride family name is an interesting play-on-words, given the way events unfold; Xavier sounds like 'saviour' when in fact his actions years ago may have caused Hester's mother great distress; 'Black Wing' the dead swan has ominous overtones; the 'blind' Catwoman, ironically, has a way of seeing and understanding events very clearly as they happen.
- **Places** – by setting the play in a bog, 'in a bleak white landscape of ice and snow', Carr prepares the ground for a chilling story in a remote and lonely place where spirits and ghosts hang close by, and where the past will come to haunt the present.
- **Father Willow** – he is a very poor minister of the faith and symbolises the uselessness of formal organised religion in giving real shape and meaning to peoples' lives. His blessing and prayers at the wedding are a sideshow to the long-winded and pretentious speeches of the parents; even his name suggests that he will bend and break in a strong wind, symbolic of the lack of influence that organised religion currently has in the country.
- **Flames** – everything 'goes up in flames' at the end, contrasting with the supposed celebration of a wedding. Also, we are left wondering if these are the flames of hell that Hester has now entered into, having just executed her only child.
- **Sunrise to sunset** – by staging the events over the course of one day, Marina Carr was following the conventions of a Greek tragedy whereby a character undergoes great suffering before realising their error and facing a noble death, all between sunrise and sunset, emphasising how quickly life can pass us by.

exam focus

Your notes on characters and themes can help you answer the 30-mark question on the day. Look at this example below.

SAMPLE QUESTION AND ANSWER (10 MARKS/8 MINUTES)

By the Bog of Cats by Marina Carr (2020/2021)

Question

Identify one challenge Hester faces because of Carthage's marriage to Caroline and explain how she responds to this challenge. Support your answer with reference to the text.

SAMPLE ANSWER

The most obvious challenge that Hester faces because of Carthage's marriage to Caroline is her own jealous rage. In fairness to Hester, it is understandable that she would be jealous. She is quite put out by the fact that her long-time lover and father of her only child has clearly rejected her. Caroline is ten years younger than Hester and from a family with considerable wealth and influence. Initially Hester explains her annoyance to Carthage and accuses him of *'selling me and Josie down the river for a few lumpy auld acres and notions of respectability'.*

Hester is also losing her home so there is a lot at stake for her. She claims a deep connection with her place of birth, despite Xavier threatening to run her out *'like a frightened hare'.* She answers back with: *'I've as much right to this place as any of yees, more, for it holds me to it in ways it has never held yees'.* Unfortunately, her decision to turn up at the actual wedding drunk and dressed in white shows her to be a pathetic figure, more to be pitied than admired. At that point, she has gone beyond any hope of overcoming the challenge of her jealous rage and the tragic end to the play follows soon afterwards.

(216 words)

EXAMINER'S ASSESSMENT

An excellent answer, providing context and supporting quotation to back up the clear points being made. Full marks deserved.

MARKS AWARDED

6 + 4 = 10/10 (O1 Grade)

4. *The Playboy of the Western World* by J. M. Synge (2020)

Storyline

The entire play is set in a pub 'on the wild coast of Mayo', some time around 1907. It has three acts.

ACT 1 – Pegeen Mike, daughter of the pub owner Michael James Flaherty, writes a list of essentials for her upcoming wedding. She is engaged to a local 'fat and fair young man' named Shawn Keogh.

- Her father and his drinking friends are attending a local wake and she makes arrangements for the wedding as Shawn looks on. Her father returns, and demands that Shawn stay overnight with Pegeen. He refuses, for fear the priest might not allow it.
- Shawn then tells of seeing a wild man in a ditch earlier that day. It turns out that this man is Christy Mahon, the young **'playboy'** of the story.
- Christy then enters the pub, quite dirty and appearing to be frightened. He tells an amazing story of being on the run, having killed his own father.
- The locals are initially very impressed by his story and he is offered a job by Michael right away.
- Pegeen instantly falls for his **charm** and she dismisses the **cowardly** Shawn from the pub.
- The Widow Quin hears of the playboy's arrival and takes great interest, but again, Pegeen sends her off.
- Pegeen's upcoming marriage disappoints the playboy, who wonders to himself why he didn't kill his father sooner, if he had known such affection and attention would come his way. He sleeps soundly.

ACT 2 – The next day, the playboy's arrival causes much **upheaval** and excitement in the village.

- He tells of how he murdered his father with a spade, as his father had demanded that he marry an ugly old widow. Local girls seek his affection, while Shawn **conspires** with the Widow Quin to try to get him to leave, even offering him money and clothes.
- He finds himself entered in the local sports day on the beach later that afternoon. However, soon after, his father, 'Old Mahon' – bandaged, bloodied but still very much alive – arrives in the village.

- The Widow sends Old Mahon off to the harbour, while she decides to try to arrange a quick marriage between Christy and Pegeen. She hopes that she will receive **privileges** in the pub from then onwards.

ACT 3 – Later that evening, news of the playboy's great feats in the local sports day are spoken of in the pub.

- Old Mahon returns once more and grows increasingly suspicious. Widow Quin convinces him that he is mad, given the bad head injury he has suffered. He leaves again, in search of Christy.

- While the crowds watch the final events on the beach, Christy proposes to Pegeen and she accepts. But her father Michael enters along with Shawn, and they insist that she must marry Shawn.

- Christy offers to fight Shawn for her, so when Shawn refuses to fight, her father changes his mind and agrees to her marriage to the playboy.

- However, Old Mahon returns once more and the truth about Christy emerges. He isn't nearly as brave and as wild as his story suggests.

- This leads to another fight between father and son and offstage we hear a loud cry and then silence. With this turn of events, the locals no longer approve of Christy so they attempt to tie him up and bring him to the police.

- Amid much violent struggling and arguing, Old Mahon crawls in yet again, this time demanding that Christy be released and promising that they both will leave Mayo forever.

- Christy refuses to leave peacefully and they both exit in serious discomfort.

- Shawn decides to remind Pegeen of her marriage arrangement with him. She boxes his ears and **laments** that she has lost the only playboy of the western world. This is the closing line of the play.

Five Key Words

- **Charm** – pleasing, appealing personality
- **Upheaval** – a sense of chaos, disturbance, trouble
- **Conspire** – to plan secretly, illegally, to work together
- **Privilege** – a special benefit, advantage or exemption
- **Lament** – a cry of pain, sadness, loss or mourning

Some important notes on revising *The Playboy of the Western World*

- This text is a **drama, written to be experienced on stage in a theatre.** If you don't get to see a live performance, it is very useful to **watch a DVD version** or watch some scenes on YouTube if possible.
- The play is full of poetic phrases and heavily accented lines. (e.g. Christy describes his murderous act: **'I just riz the loy and let fall the edge of it on his skull.'**) This can make it a little difficult to read. However, an **audio version of the text** will make it much easier to understand.
- Synge chose to write this play based upon his experiences with people from the **Aran Islands** and other places in the West of Ireland.
- He was criticised heavily at the time by some Irish critics. Some felt that he was patronising and poking fun at the supposed **backwardness of Irish country people**, especially rural Catholics. Synge himself was a middle-class Protestant, born in Wicklow. He said that **the play was based on 'a true story'.**

CHARACTERS

There are twelve characters, plus some 'peasants' listed in the cast. The most complex characters are the ones to focus on:

- Christy Mahon
- Pegeen Mike
- the Widow Quin

These three characters provide us with many insights and important quotes from the play. The other characters (the 'girls' and the 'farmers', etc.) tend to provide background noise and observations, but not much that is very significant for revision.

1) Christy Mahon – playboy or chancer?

- He is the **handsome and charming 'playboy'**, aged in his twenties. He is on the run because he has murdered his father, Old Mahon.
- He **earns the affection of his hosts** rather quickly, especially Pegeen Mike, to whom he is then briefly engaged.
- The locals love his **rebellious spirit**. His life seems to be the **opposite of their dull, boring and predictable lives.**
- He is a **fine athlete** and demonstrates great skills at the local sports day, much to the local girls' enjoyment.
- He cannot believe his **luck** by the end of Act 1 to have *'two fine women fighting for the likes of me.'* He wonders why he didn't kill his father before now.
- He represents the **freedom and adventure that many of the local people would love to have.** However, Christy is nowhere near as brave and dashing as he makes himself out to be.

- Old Mahon calls Christy:

  'a dirty, stuttering lout'

  'a liar on walls, a talker of folly, a man you'd see stretched the half of the day in the brown ferns with his belly to the sun'

  'drunk on the smell of a pint'

- By the end, he has attempted to kill his father a total of three times, without success.

- Mike's attitude also changes towards him, calling him a *'lousy schemer' and a 'frisky rascal'.*

- He leaves in disgrace, dragging his father with him, but not before biting Shawn in the leg and cursing everybody around for the way things have worked out.

Conclusion

- He is far from heroic and more likely what we would call a **'chancer'** in today's language.

2) Pegeen Mike – the love interest

- She speaks one of the most important lines in the play: *'there's a great gap between a gallous story and a dirty deed.'* This summarises a central question of the play: is Christy Mahon a character to be admired or to be despised?

- Synge sets this question up via the notion of marriage. Would a **fine country girl**, daughter of a publican and businessman, truly want to marry such a man?

- Pegeen, aged in her twenties, is no doubt a **strong-willed and quick-thinking young woman**. She has a rebellious and independent streak, being quick to challenge Church authority, at least while standing in her own public house.

- She tells Shawn to *'stop tormenting me with Father Reilly'* and she wittily remarks that the Pope *'wouldn't bother with this place'.*

- She is well able to challenge Christy, the playboy, and doubts his story from the start: *'A soft lad the like of you wouldn't slit the windpipe of a screeching sow.'*

- For Pegeen Mike, she faces a future that is either a dull, loveless marriage to Shawn, or something more adventurous and exotic in an attachment to the playboy: *'Wouldn't it be a bitter thing for a girl to go marrying the like of Shawneen, and he a middling kind of scarecrow, with no savagery or fine words in him at all?'*

- When she then realises the lies that Christy has told, and when she sees the real 'savagery' of father and son brawling, she faces the reality that the playboy, the *'ugly liar, was playing off the hero, and the fright of men.'*

Pegeen Mike – Protagonist 'The Love Interest'	Widow Quin – Antagonist 'The Love Rival'
• attractive	• scheming
• strong-willed	• manipulative
• quick-thinking	• experienced
• organised	• shrewd
• rebellious	• realistic
• independent	• cynical
• witty	• lonely
• outspoken	
• disappointed	

3) The Widow Quin – the 'older woman' and love rival?

- A woman of 'about thirty', her widowed status meant that she had considerable 'experience' in terms of life's hardships and realities.
- She acts as an **antagonist** in the play, causing mischief, trying to keep one step ahead of Pegeen and Christy and **manipulating others to her advantage**.
- She sees herself as a suitable wife for the playboy, having supposedly killed her own husband. She is the **'love rival'** initially once the playboy arrives.
- However, she sees that marriage is unlikely so she then turns to helping Christy marry Pegeen in return for favours in the pub.
- She also acts as a role model for the young girls of the play, with her **cunning scheming** and her ability to manipulate Old Mahon, among others.
- She is motivated by **desperation** and the awful prospect of **loneliness**. She will do anything to have a reliable man with her to bring stability and steady income to her household.
- She is still young enough to have numerous children and therefore can be played on stage as a **seductive 'older woman'**, rather than a bitter old widow.
- Nothing works out for her in the end, however. As she leaves the stage in Act 3, she remarks that *'It's in the madhouse they should put him, not the jail,'* as the playboy is led away.

Other Characters

The following characters are quite important but are not as complex as the ones above. They are more 'one-dimensional':

- **Old Mahon**
- **Mike Flaherty**
- **Shawn Keogh**

Old Mahon makes a number of appearances and suffers near-death three times in the play.

- **He is the walking embodiment of the lies that Christy tells.** They reconcile just as they are both kicked out of the village.
- However, the play closes with the suggestion that the son has now taken over the dominant position in the family. **Christy calls his father the 'heathen slave'** as they leave.
- The failure of Old Mahon to earn the respect of his son is considered a moral failure on the part of Old Mahon.
- The **violence** that they bring with them is quite real, much less heroic than the tales and legends that they are fond of spreading.

Mike Flaherty is a central character of any rural Irish village, being a publican.

- However, he spends a considerable length of time in the play in various states of drunkenness.
- The drama on his doorstep, and the apparent wildness of his daughter's desires, suggest that he has **lost a grip on authority.** He is not really respected by her.
- In urging Christy and Shawn to literally 'fight for his daughter's hand in marriage,' he demonstrates a level of savagery and brutality that was a source of controversy when the play was first staged.

Shawn Keogh is a **simple, one-dimensional young farmer,** typical of the times.

- He is portrayed in an unflattering light. He is **weak-minded, lacking imagination and terrified of what the priest or bishop might think of him.** He is cowardly, almost to the point of comedy.
- Pegeen boxes his ears at the end, symbolising a lack of connection or attraction between them. It would make their upcoming marriage seem all the more ridiculous.

Themes

1) Family Values

The play asks questions of traditional family values and gender roles at the time.

- All three significant family units suffer from some sort of absence: a) there is no 'Mrs Flaherty' mentioned, so we must assume that Pegeen's mother is dead; b) there is no 'Mrs Mahon' either, for reasons unknown; c) a widow plays a central part in the action.
- When the family unit is damaged or incomplete, it causes difficulty and uncertainty. Rural Irish village life was built upon strong family bonds and values, reinforced by the dominant hand of the Catholic Church. When these things are out of kilter, trouble is bound to happen.
- The Playboy takes advantage of this loose sense of family values. He quickly discovers that a wide range of females – not just Pegeen and the Widow Quin, but also Honor, Sarah, Nelly and Susan – are intrigued by his charms. His interference with the

upcoming wedding plans can be seen as partly because the family units and family values of the village are not upheld strongly enough to put him back in his place.

- The reality for most people in the play is quite simple: life is quite miserable, whereby they are stuck in an environment where one is expected to follow a simple path. Men farm the land, drink and play sports to relax. Women get married at the earliest opportunity and settle into a life of child-rearing and drudgery as 'farmers' wives'. Gossip and illusions of romance fill the women's minds to kill the time. Nothing too exciting happens. The Catholic Church oversees this strict social order, and disobedience – as Shawn tells us regularly – will be punished.

2) Violence and Cruelty

It is remarkable that the village as a whole seems to celebrate the virtue of murdering one's father.

- The playboy 'murderer' is seen as a hero. He is also made a hero at the local sports day. By demonstrating a type of manliness, along with quick wit and poetic charm, the playboy conforms to a basic **stereotype of an ideal boyfriend** and potential husband.
- However, when we see the violence and anger between Christy and Old Mahon 'for real' in Act 3, we get a better reflection of their character. It is no longer a great story but a **bloody and gruesome reality**.
- In order to make life more bearable, the people develop a tremendous sense of imagination and colour in their language and interactions. Many of their observations are **funny but also cruel and sarcastic**. There are countless examples of this in the play and each can be read as an indication of the harshness and cruelty in the minds and hearts of the characters.

Examples

- PEGEEN: *'Marcus Quin, God rest him, got six months for maiming ewes, and he a great warrant to tell stories of Holy Ireland till he'd have the old women shedding down tears about their feet.'* (scolding Shawn for suggesting that there were no 'sinners' in the village)
- SHAWN: *'I'm after feeling a kind of fellow in the furzy ditch, groaning wicked like a maddening dog.'* (upon seeing the playboy on the road earlier)
- MIKE: *'Pegeen, you'll have no call to be spying after if you've a score of young girls weeding in your fields!'* (assuring Pegeen that Shawn is the right man for her)
- CHRISTY: *'I never left my own parish till Tuesday was a week.'* (the playboy's poetic way of saying how long he has been on the run)
- OLD MAHON: *'If he seen a red petticoat coming swinging over the hill, he'd be off to hide in the sticks, and you'd see him shooting out his sheep's eyes between the little twigs and the leaves, and his two ears rising like a hare looking out through a gap. Girls indeed!'* (telling of Christy's true behaviours around young women)

There are many other examples – all of them expressing a great deal of colour and imagination as people try to escape the dull, boring life they actually lead.

SAMPLE QUESTION AND ANSWER (10 MARKS/8 MINUTES)

The Playboy of the Western World by J. M. Synge (2020)

Question

What does the Widow Quin think of Christy Mahon at the end of the play? Explain briefly and quote from the play.

SAMPLE ANSWER

> When Christie leaves the village at the end of the play, the Widow Quin passes a comment about him and his father, Old Mahon. She says that 'It's in the madhouse they should put him, not the jail.' I think she is actually disappointed by the fact that he didn't fall for her earlier in the play. She tried to seduce him early on and she talked about how good a farmer she was. But Christy didn't really take much interest in her, so by the end of it all she does not care much for him. She is probably a bit jealous too and maybe lonely because she is a widow and for her, a new husband would be very useful for the future.
>
> (125 words)

EXAMINER'S ASSESSMENT

The candidate includes **three possible responses**: disappointed, jealous and lonely. All have some merit but it would be better to **focus more closely** on one or maybe two of these, with supporting reference or quotation. There is sufficient knowledge of the play and the language and mechanics are quite good, so a solid answer, just short of top marks.

MARKS AWARDED

4 + 4 = 8/10 (O2 Grade)

5. *Room* by Emma Donoghue (2020/2021)

Storyline

This novel tells a very dark and disturbing story. It is loosely based on real events, which makes the story even more shocking.

- The narrator of the story is a boy named Jack. It begins on his fifth birthday. He lives with his mother, who he calls 'Ma', in 'Room', a locked outbuilding containing a small kitchen, a bath and toilet, a wardrobe, a bed, a rug, a TV set and some basic materials. Jack believes that only Room and the things it contains (including himself and Ma) are 'real'. Ma convinces Jack to believe that the rest of the world, or 'Outside', exists only on television. She tries her best to keep Jack healthy and happy and manages a very strict and organised routine for him. She also breastfeeds him regularly.

- 'Old Nick' visits Room at night while Jack sleeps hidden in the wardrobe. Old Nick brings them food and basic things needed to survive. Jack is unaware that Old Nick kidnapped Ma when she was nineteen years old and has kept her locked in Room for the past seven years. Old Nick sexually assaults and rapes Ma regularly. She became pregnant and gave birth to a girl but the baby died while being born. Shortly afterwards, she gave birth to Jack.

- Ma learns that Old Nick has been unemployed for the past six months and is in danger of losing his home. Ma comes up with a plan to get Jack out of Room because she fears that Old Nick might kill them. She pretends that Jack has died and convinces Old Nick to remove him, wrapped in a rug, from Room. Jack then escapes Old Nick and manages to reach a friendly stranger, who contacts the police. He manages to convince the police to find Ma and free her from Room, which they do shortly afterwards.

- Mother and son slowly come to terms with the outside world. It is extremely difficult for both of them to adjust. After a television interview ends badly, Ma suffers a mental breakdown and attempts suicide.

- Jack then goes to live with his grandmother and her new partner for several days. Without the security of his mother, Jack becomes even more confused by his surroundings, including his new extended family. He also becomes more troubled and frightened by his mother's changing personality as she tries to adjust to life. He wants to keep her for himself.

- Finally, Jack cuts his long hair and looks to visit Room once more. He and Ma return to the scene of their captivity, but Jack no longer feels any connection to it. The story ends as he says his goodbyes, touching all of the familiar objects and walls, before he and Ma leave Room together for the final time.

Five Key Words

- **Exposition** – the beginning, introduction, start
- **Complication** – when things go wrong, unwanted changes occur
- **Climax** – the high-point, when tension is at its most heightened
- **Reversal** – when things turn around, a backlash
- **Resolution** – how something ends, resolved, concluded, finished

Some important notes for revising *Room*

- The entire story is told from the **point of view** of a five-year-old. He is the eyes and ears of everything that happens.
- Jack describes things **literally**. (e.g. Jeep; Remote; Meltedy Spoon; Wordy Ball; Skylight; Baby Jesus, etc.) He sees the world as five-year-olds do: in clear, concrete terms, but with a tremendous curiosity.
- This means that many plot details and situations are hinted at and suggested. It **creates a very uncomfortable atmosphere** at times. Perhaps the most disturbing example is how Jack counts the creaks of the bed that are made when Old Nick is assaulting Ma.
- The award-winning film version of the novel is worth watching. But remember that **a film will always be different** to a written text. It tells the story from many angles, unlike the novel.
- It is important to **learn key quotations from the text** and not to rely too heavily on the film.

Five-Part Story

There are five long chapters in the novel. This is similar to a Shakespearean play with five acts:

1) Introduction ('PRESENTS') – we meet Jack, Ma, Old Nick and discover the horror of the situation.
2) Complication ('UNLYING') – Ma is forced to slowly reveal to Jack the truth about 'Outside' and why they are here in Room.
3) Dramatic Climax ('DYING') – Jack escapes from Room by pretending to be dead.
4) Further Complications ('AFTER') – Jack and Ma struggle to adapt and are separated following Ma's attempted suicide.
5) Conclusion ('LIVING') – Jack and Ma are re-united and then visit Room one last time to say goodbye.

A 'Key Moment' in each chapter

1. The first time Jack describes the 'beep-beep' as Old Nick enters Room that night.
2. Jack sees a plane through the skylight and shouts that 'Outside' must be real.
3. Jack escapes in Rug. This episode should be read as one long piece (it is very important).
4. The TV interview – Ma tells their story.
5. Jack cuts his pony-tail and looks forward to meeting Ma again (read from this point to the end).

CHARACTERS

So much of the novel revolves around **Ma** and **Jack**. So in the exam, it is likely that some questions will focus on their relationship and how things change. Here are some broad points about the two of them:

1) Ma

We never get to know her full name but she is portrayed as a truly extraordinary woman.

Ma's Life Story

- She was originally adopted by her parents (Grandma and Grandpa) who are now separated; Grandma's new partner is named Leo.
- She has a brother called Paul, who is married to Deana. They have a child named Bronwyn.
- She describes herself in the interview as 'ordinary' as a child.
- She had an abortion at the age of eighteen.
- She was abducted by Old Nick at nineteen, imprisoned in Room and raped repeatedly.
- She became pregnant with a baby girl who died from suffocation and a lack of proper care during birth.
- The following year, she gave birth to Jack – alone – in Room; the stains from the birth remain on Rug throughout. Jack is attached to the rug and it is an important item for them both.
- She creates the world of 'Room' so that Jack does not have to think about the situation 'Outside'.
- She teaches him everything he needs to know: language, numbers, prayers, hygiene, exercise. She devotes her entire time to keeping him occupied, while trying not to lose her sanity.
- She once tried to kill Old Nick with the lid of the toilet; he broke her wrist in return. She never tried to overpower him after that. She became 'polite'.
- She suffers occasional mental breakdowns and unconsciousness: Jack calls this 'gone'.
- The relationship changes when Jack reaches the age of five. She cannot continue to deny him the truth: *'What we see on TV is ... it's pictures of real things.'*
- She makes the decision to fake Jack's death in order to try to escape.
- By doing this she knows that both of their lives are in danger. If it fails, she will likely die an appalling death by starvation.

Ma's Key Moment in the Novel

The TV interview goes very badly. Although she finds it very difficult and has a breakdown, she does tell us many important things:

- Everything she did was for Jack.
- They were never bored together.
- Having a child for herself 'saved' her – she felt that she was 'somebody' and that she was 'alive again'.
- She did everything with Old Nick on 'auto-pilot'.
- Everything was about 'keeping Jack safe'.
- When the world was eleven-foot square, everything was easier to control.
- Doing these things was simply 'being a mother'.
- She insists that they 'escaped' and were not 'rescued'.
- They did it together.

This interview, which appears in the chapter called 'After' is a very important piece of revision. It allows Ma to explain everything from her point of view. This is reported by Jack as narrator – but we get to hear Ma's inner feelings and experiences without Jack interpreting them for us.

- The TV interviewer, and the media in general, want to portray their own version of the story, that somehow Jack and Ma are disturbed and traumatised by being together in this way.
- Ma resists this furiously. It causes her to have a nervous breakdown, meaning Jack must live with his relatives for a time.
- She stops breastfeeding Jack near the end of the novel. This is a major change for Jack but signals the start of a new independent existence, still together, but this time outside of Room.

A True Heroine

The character of Ma is **resilient, creative, patient, caring, understanding, determined, proud** and, in the words of Jack, she has a face that is the *'beautifullest of them all'*. She suffers unspeakable emotional trauma. In spite of this, she is without doubt **a most heroic and admirable young woman, worthy of great praise for what she did.**

2) Jack

The story begins on Jack's fifth birthday.

Jack's Life Story

- Despite what one might expect, he is very similar to most boys of his age:
  - He asks lots of questions.
  - He likes to play games and take exercise.
  - He has a great imagination and likes hearing stories and singing songs.
  - He likes his routine, gets upset if it is disturbed, and is very interested in numbers and counting things properly.

- Naturally, he is incredibly attached to Ma and their separation is very challenging for him.
- He is very thoughtful and kind to his mother, even when she is 'gone' and he is alone and afraid.
- In fact he is quite gifted in a number of ways: his skill with numbers; his memory for poems, stories, songs and prayers; his skills of observation (he notices the mouse and the aeroplane) are excellent.
- Also, he sees the world in concrete terms. He is at an age when that is slowly changing, so trying to understand the adult way of speaking and behaving in 'Outside' is very complicated to him.

Jack's Key Moment in the Novel

- However, his greatest achievement is in managing to escape by playing dead, even to the point of going to the toilet on himself in fear, seriously hurting his knees and getting bitten by a dog, yet not giving away the truth to Old Nick.
- He is just as heroic as Ma; he overcomes the challenge of escaping Old Nick. That is an amazing feat for a five-year-old.
- He overhears something important: '*... like a newborn in many ways, despite his remarkably accelerated literacy and numeracy.*'
  Dr Clay makes this important observation shortly after Jack is admitted for analysis. But because his mother has done an incredible job in raising him, we do not view Jack as being seriously disturbed, wild or 'feral'.
- He has an uneasy relationship with his grandparents, especially Grandpa, who can hardly bear to look at him at first. Grandma does her best but seems to lack empathy and care, despite raising two of her own children.
- He is christened 'Miracle Jack' and 'Bonsai Boy' by the media, a term that Jack thinks is stupid since '*I am not a tree. I am a boy.*' Later on, as the doctors refer to five-year-olds as being 'like plastic', he once again needs to point out that '*I am a boy.*'
- The fact that he has long hair means that he is mistaken for a girl, another point that annoys him.

Jack's Reaction to 'Outsiders'

- In general, Jack can't really understand the way people in 'Outside' think and speak and he makes one of the funniest and most ironic statements of the whole novel: '*Outsiders don't understand anything, I wonder do they watch too much television?*'
- This suggests that he needs to develop an identity for himself in 'Outside', since other people keep trying to do it for him. The only person who can really help him do this is Ma. Near the end, as he is full of questions, she says to him: '*I will always call you Jack.*'

- When he finally cuts his hair and stops breast feeding, it signals a change in Jack's outlook as he now becomes more comfortable with living in 'Outside'.
- The visit one last time to Room, which now seems so much smaller and uninteresting, signals the real start of his new life together forever with Ma.
- He is just as much the hero of the story as Ma is and is also deserving of great praise.

Other Characters

- **Old Nick** plays his part as the **brutally cruel villain.**
  — We only get some glimpses of him and occasional phrases, recited by Jack as narrator.
  — The 'Room' scenario is enough to convince us that he is a thoroughly awful man, utterly evil in what he is doing.
  — At one stage, he says: *'I figure there must be something wrong ... you've never let me get a good look since the day he was born. Poor little freak's got two heads or something.'*
  — He has created a sick, twisted sense of normality and cannot understand why Jack does not accept him.
  — He is caught by the police and we assume he will spend the rest of his life, ironically enough, in a locked cell.
- **Grandma, Steppa, Grandad, Paul** and **Deana** all struggle to relate to Jack as they all enforce their understanding of how things are done in 'Outside'. For example, Jack's trip to the toy store and Grandma's horror at breastfeeding are two good examples of how these adults don't properly understand his needs and end up causing distress for him.
- However, **Officer Oh** (a local policewoman), **Noreen** (an experienced Irish nurse) and **Dr Clay** (the main therapist to Ma) all seem much kinder and understanding towards both Ma and Jack.
- Another neighbour named **Ajeet** is the one who first comes across Jack and he does the correct thing in contacting the police.

Themes

1) Love

The novel is about the triumph of a mother's love in the face of unspeakable cruelty. It is a story of how love does, after all, conquer evil.

Examples of Love Triumphing

- There is great triumph in the fact that Ma has managed to create a relatively 'normal' life for Jack in Room.
- It is also triumphant that Jack is such a loving, caring and otherwise fairly 'normal' boy, who can also show love back to his mother and, eventually, other people.
- Ma recounts how she gave birth to him alone; she refused to let Old Nick see the birth and managed to keep both herself and her new baby healthy without any post-natal or medical care.
- She is extremely defensive and protective of him in the early stages after release. She tries to assure the doctors that Jack is actually fine: *'He's never been out of my sight and nothing happened to him, nothing like you are insinuating.'*
- Jack is quite healthy, intelligent and enjoys a sound routine. This is entirely down to the tremendous sacrifice and love that Ma afforded to Jack in Room.
- Ma tells her father that Jack *'is the world to me'.* On first seeing Jack, he is lost for words and just utters *'No offence'*, which is probably quite an offensive thing to say in the circumstances.

- The character of Grandpa does not seem the type to respond in the same loving way as Ma does, and blames 'jet lag' for his thinking.
- Ma goes on to explain her love and commitment to Jack in the TV interview. The interviewer asks a question that upsets Ma: she suggests that Ma must *'stand guard between your son and the world.'* Ma responds by saying: *'Yeah, it's called being a mother.'*
- In other words, Ma is saying that any loving mother would do the same. However, very few would be capable of such love and of holding the relationship and their whole world together in the circumstances. Ma does this very successfully for five years.
- **Jack is just as defensive about Ma.** He keeps one of her rotten teeth with him at all times when she is away, even sticking it in his mouth to keep it safe. It is his little way of staying connected to Ma.
- He is also very attached to 'Rug', the way children can be attached to blankets or teddy bears. It is once again his five-year-old way of showing what matters in life.
- What matters most of all is that Ma and himself are together and happy.

- **Steppa** is quite sarcastic at times and suggests to Jack that Ma must know nothing about plumbing. Jack delivers a lovely response, typical of a five-year-old: *'Ma knows about everything.'*
- **The love between Ma and Jack is what lights up the novel.** Any study of this novel cannot miss the theme of love running through it.

2) The World 'Outside'

A strong theme of the novel is that **the modern world of today can be a scary place.**

- 'Outside' is the world of Old Nick. He lives there comfortably enough and is able to inflict unbelievable cruelty for many years without anybody knowing.
- 'Outside' is also a world where *'people are locked up in all sorts of ways'*, according to Ma. She speaks of babies being tied to cots and prisoners in solitary confinement among other things. She suggests that the world is full of cruelty and suffering and she isn't a 'saint' just because she raised Jack inside Room.
- Their escape also disrupts the routine and 'normality' of Ma and Jack. She has her first proper shower in seven years and tells Jack that *'we don't have to do things as we used to.'*
- But Jack *'likes breakfast before bath'*. She has to stop breastfeeding and Jack must realise that saying and doing certain things and touching people inappropriately, for example, is not acceptable.
- Ma explains the difference between Room and Outside during the interview. She says at one stage that *'when our world was 11-foot square it was easier to control.'* This has a double meaning: Old Nick gets to control their movements but also Ma and Jack get to control how they act together inside there, without any other distractions and influences. Jack also notices the wastefulness of people 'outside' who seem to need enormous amounts of 'stuff' to get through daily life: *'They've got a million of things and different kinds of each thing, like all kinds of chocolate bars and machines and shoes.'* There is an unstated theme here that people can get by together on very little once they learn to value the little that they have.
- Another thing Ma realises on escaping Room is that they are now reluctant 'celebrities'. This is the type of attention neither she nor Jack wants. Her lawyer Morris tries to advise on how best to prepare for the future. He suggests the TV interview and Ma answers: *'You think we should sell ourselves before somebody else does.'*
- Later Jack has to run indoors from the park as a number of paparazzi reporters in helicopters try to get a glimpse of him. His uncle Paul also struggles to disguise Jack's identity when in public, which causes more confusion for Jack.
- Outside, therefore, is a world where everything is for sale, even the most private intimate details of your most personal intimate relationships.

exam focus

Your notes on characters and themes can help you answer the short 10-mark question on the day. Look at the example on the next page.

SAMPLE QUESTION AND ANSWER (10 MARKS/8 MINUTES)

Room by Emma Donoghue (2020/2021)

Question

Explain what happens when Ma and Jack meet Grandpa for the first time. Refer to the text in support of your answer.

SAMPLE ANSWER

The first meeting of the family does not go well. Grandpa has just come off a flight and he says that he has jet-lag. On seeing Jack, he mutters 'no offence'. It is as if he cannot accept what has happened. This is a terrible thing to say in my opinion. Jack as usual does not understand when the adults use words like 'he' and 'me' so he gets confused at this time. Ma on the other hand explodes with anger and reminds her father that Jack 'is the world to me'. It is a sad moment for Ma once again because it shows us that people in 'outside' find it really difficult to adapt to the needs of Ma and her son Jack. Her father can't even say he is glad to see her in this moment.

(138 words)

EXAMINER'S ASSESSMENT

This is a concise and detailed answer that addresses the question and demonstrates good knowledge of the moment in question. Two accurate quotations with following explanation, well-phrased with good vocabulary, mean that this will score highly in the exam.

MARKS AWARDED

6 + 4 = 10/10 (O1 Grade)

6. *Philadelphia, Here I Come!* by Brian Friel (2021)

Storyline

The play concerns a young Irishman, **Gareth** or **'Gar' O'Donnell**, who lives in the village of **Ballybeg, Donegal** with his father **S.B. O'Donnell** and the housekeeper **Madge**. His mother died giving birth to him. It is the eve of his departure for Philadelphia, where he

wants to make a new life for himself. The story is told in a series of **flashbacks**, as well as through Gar's fantasies about the bright future he hopes to have in America.

- Gar is presented to us as **two individual characters**, played by two different actors, representing his **public and private** selves. These two have very different personalities: Public Gar is **the man who is seen** and who interacts with the other characters in the play. Private Gar represents **Gar's inner thoughts and feelings** and he can only interact with Public Gar.

- We learn of his conflicting feelings about leaving Ballybeg, which represents for him **both the positive and negative aspects of the life he has lived**. The play teases out these thoughts and issues over the course of an evening and early the next morning, in three distinct episodes.

Episode 1

- Gar dances with Madge as he **excitedly thinks of leaving**. When he moves to his room, he speaks with Private Gar and they act out some imagined scenarios about his future life in America.

- His father, S.B., calls for him. **Public responds angrily, which has become a habit.** Public then quietly begins to think about his mother, Maire, and his ex-girlfriend, Kate, two important people from his past.

- We discover that his proposal of marriage to Kate, the daughter of a senator, fell apart as he wasn't deemed financially stable enough. She married a local doctor instead. Private teases him by saying '***Honeymoon in Mallorca and you couldn't afford to take her to Malahide***'.

- Over tea with his father, Private makes fun of the way S.B. lives his life in such a boring way. As they eat their tea, Gar's old schoolteacher, **Master Boyle**, arrives and gives him some advice about how to act in America, saying '***You're doing the right thing of course. You'll never regret it***'.

- Despite his good intentions to visit, he ends up asking Gar for money to buy a drink at the pub. As he is leaving, he tells Gar that he'll miss him and **Gar begins to have doubts about leaving Ballybeg after all**.

Episode 2

- Gar is lying on his bed. Private tries to distract Public from having thoughts about staying at home. Gradually, the conversation turns to **Aunt Lizzy**, Gar's aunt who invites him to stay with her in Philadelphia.

- The scene turns back to the past when Aunt Lizzy, her husband **Con** and their friend **Ben** visit Gar. Lizzy is a loud, dominant character, while Ben and Con remain silent for the majority of the time. She reveals that she is unable to have children of her own and **begs Gar to come live with them in America**.

- When the scene flashes back to the present, Gar's group of friends, **Ned, Tom and Joe visit**. But no-one except Joe brings up his departure, suggesting that they actually don't care much for him.

- However, as a parting gift, Ned gives Gar a leather belt. Kate visits soon after and they have a pleasant, courteous conversation. But it stirs up Gar's feelings, so much so that he curses the locals as '*asylum cases, the whole bloody lot of them*'. He is more determined than ever to leave.

Episode 3

- This episode occurs in two short scenes before and after midnight. Gar, Madge and S.B. are praying, but Private Gar **begins recalling a pleasant memory from the past**. He remembers himself and S.B. on a boat when he was younger.

- When Public asks S.B. about it, they are interrupted by the Canon's arrival. **The Canon** is the parish priest in Ballybeg. He and S.B. begin playing a board game, much to the annoyance of Private, who complains at length about how the Canon is supposed to be a person of wisdom, but instead does not do his job very well.

- In the final part, S.B. is sitting at the dining table and staring at Gar's door. They attempt to connect with each other over old stories, but **father and son never manage to exchange their feelings**.

- When S.B. leaves, Gar comes out to meet Madge. They say goodnight to each other, and as Madge walks away, Private asks Public why he has to leave, to which Public replies that **he doesn't know**.

Five Key Words

- **Screwballs** – the nickname that Gar secretly gives his father
- **Eejiting** – rural Irish slang for stupid, childish behaviour
- **Bugger** – an annoyance, either in a person or in action
- **Lock, stock and barrel** – slang for 'everything', particularly one's business assets
- **Wee** – Northern Irish slang for 'small', an affectionate term for children

CHARACTERS

1) Gar Public

- Gar Public is the main character of the play. He appears to be **introverted, generally polite and likeable**. The fact that a former teacher, former girlfriend, three male friends and the parish priest all visit to see him off the night before is testament to his general good character and status in the village. He is a **thoughtful** individual, constantly balancing thoughts of his troubled past with opportunities for a better future.

- But his shortcomings are quickly made obvious in the play. He is eager to escape the limitations of life in Ireland but does **not really have any clear plan** or reason for doing so. He is also **unable to communicate these desires** to his father and therefore chooses to be short-tempered and gruff. His failure to win

Kate's heart stems partly from his financial status: selling eggs to hotels does not meet her parent's expectations. It also points to his naive nature and a lack of certainty about his future. His supposed friends, Ned, Tom and Joe, are of little help as they behave immaturely – chasing women and drinking without much care. The play follows Gar Public as he considers his move from one type of life to another.

2) Gar Private

- Friel creates an 'alter-ego' character who is quite deliberately the opposite of Public. He expresses Gar's secret thoughts, opinions and wishes. He is **extroverted, quick-witted, full of confidence and at times, outlandish**. It makes him the most enjoyable character to observe on stage. His sharp criticism, especially of Public Gar, is a recurring feature of the play. A good example is the near harassment of Public in Episode 1 as he fondly remembers a song associated with Kate: '*Tell me randy boy, tell me the truth: have you got over that sickness? Do you still love her? Do you still lust after her? Well do you? Do You? Do You?*' There are also times where Private can become overwhelmed with emotion, causing him to recite a speech to calm himself down. It shows that Gar is troubled and full of emotional energy that needs a route for expression. **Private seeks genuine connections with others, representing the pent-up emotion of Gar himself.** Most especially, he's desperate to form a relationship with S.B. and constantly urges Public to '*say something*'. He sounds like the more developed version of Gar, who is wise enough to note that the three young friends are little more than '*ignorant louts*'. Private voice urging Public to make the first move and open up to S.B. in the final episode.

3) S.B.

- **S.B. O'Donnell** is a widower and shopkeeper in the town of Ballybay. In his late sixties, he is described in the notes as a '*responsible, respectable citizen*' who is content to dress well, tend to his small shop and generally not get too involved in anything remotely exciting in life. He appears to have **closed himself off** from having to think too deeply about life in general, being initially preoccupied by whether it was '*two or three rolls of barbed wire*' that arrived in the van that morning. **The tension between his only son Gar and himself, is the source of much of the drama in the play.** Indeed, much of the plot emerges from the mind of Gar via flashback, as well as through the occasional memories and stories that S.B. exchanges with Madge, Master Boyle and the Canon. **His memory of Young Gar in his sailor suit** is one rare, poignant moment where we see him attempt to express his feelings for his son.

- Gar's decision to leave for Philadelphia ultimately **forces him to re-think what has been routine for him for many years now**, including how to deal with it emotionally. There is a strong hint that his world is about to change drastically and he isn't fully aware of what to do about it. He mentions to Madge in the final scene that *'It's different now. I'll manage by myself now. Eh? I'll manage fine, eh?'* The uncertainty in his voice is what leaves us fearful for his future, now that his only son is potentially gone forever.

4) Madge

- **Madge** is the **housekeeper** and has worked for S.B. for many years. She evidently feels comfortable around the two and in the true spirit of the **'maternal'** character, is **emotionally aware and deeply concerned** for both S.B. and Gar. She is **talkative and friendly**, a hostess to visitors who drop into the O'Donnell home or shop and a reliable employee.

- Madge is the closest to a mother figure for Gar, but is **not a substitute mother**. In fact, she is slow to reveal much about Gar's mother and is **reluctant to speak much of the past**, knowing it will potentially cause tension. Madge's daughter has just had a child and has promised to name it after her. When Madge finally leaves the O'Donnell residence to see her new grandchild she learns that her daughter and son-in-law have decided to name the baby Brigid instead. She is slightly disappointed but understands. She plays the part of the **patient and wise observer**. She knows of the tensions between father and son, but rather than trying to fix things, she is there to listen to the two men in their attempts to come to terms with both their past and future. It is interesting that **Gar's final image and memory of his home on his final night is Madge**, not his father, confirming her importance in his life to that point.

Themes

1) Family Relationships

The theme of relationships, especially within the family, is central to this play. The **father–son relationship** is the most interesting.

- Gar is unable to communicate with his father, and vice-versa. We see that Gar Private spends the entire play calling him names like *'Screwballs'* behind his back, when in reality, **all he wants is for his father to ask him to stay**. His father, though, is emotionally distant, which causes much of the tension in the play and the main reason why he wants to emigrate to Philadelphia.

- **Madge** is the housekeeper, the go-between and **the maternal figure of the household**. It is through Madge that we learn how Gar's mother died and that S. B. does have feelings, even though he is not able to express them fully.

- We also learn through Madge that Gar and his father are *'as like as two peas'* and escaping to Philadelphia will not solve any of Gar's problems: *'And when he's the age of the boss, he'll turn out just the same. And although I won't be here to see it, you'll find he's learned nothin' in between time.'*

- Gar and his father are quite similar, in that they are **both afraid to express themselves emotionally** and are almost embarrassed in one another's company. Gar recounts the day when he went fishing with his father as a young boy on Lough na Cloc Cor. However, his father has no memory of it.

- We listen to S.B.'s own story from the past, when he brought Gar to school on his first day in his *'wee sailor suit'*. Both characters yearn to be loved and understood, but despite almost coming together at the end, they remain emotionally distant.

- The **tragedy** of the play is that there is no resolution to this father-son dilemma. Gar goes to Philadelphia without coming to terms with the problems in their relationship. His final sight before he leaves is of Madge, not his father and as Private asks why he has to do it, Public Gar can only say *'I don't know'*.

2) Public v Private Life

This play presents the idea that people can carry with them both a public and a private self. Whatever we see on the outside, **there might lurk a very different aspect to a person on the inside**. It suggests that we might hide our true feelings, often at a cost to our relationships. This is a significant theme of the play.

- **Public** is quiet and sometimes short-tempered with his father, but generally he **avoids confrontation** or loose comment. On the other hand, **Private** is full of energy and sarcasm, especially towards his father, who he harshly criticises throughout the book. **He often gets carried away**, such as his outlandish ridicule of the Canon in Episode 3. He provides numerous comical moments in the play. **It is impossible to see Public acting in this way**, therefore strongly suggesting that the difference between our public and private selves can be quite significant.

- Also, the fact that Gar wants to escape to America hints at a desire for a different type of life, **a different 'public' version of himself**, away from the repressive and quite 'boring' Ballybeg in Catholic Ireland. He is conflicted by the idea of lust and even calls himself a *'sex maniac'*. He constantly pictures scenes involving himself and an imaginary woman.

- There are strong suggestions that life in America is exciting. It is a place that Gar hopes will allow a bit more of the 'private' Gar to emerge. In Ballybeg, **Public Gar is followed around by past mistakes and losses** as well as a lack of communication with his father. Even though he does not really know why he is leaving, his private self urges him onwards regardless.

exam focus

Your notes on characters and themes can help you answer the 30-mark question on the day. Look at the example on the next page.

SAMPLE QUESTION AND ANSWER (10 MARKS/8 MINUTES)

Philadelphia, Here I Come! by Brian Friel (2021)

Question

In your opinion, was Gar a good son to S.B. O'Donnell? Give reasons for your answer.

SAMPLE ANSWER

I do think that Gar was a good son to S.B. even though he leaves him at the end. He tries to be a caring son, but is quite immature and unwise, something his father finds disappointing. We see a glimpse of his immaturity in the first flashback to when his relationship with Kate fails. He sounds like a silly, young fool with little understanding of life and love. This adds up to a young man with emotional problems and a lack of confidence. However, what makes him a good son is that despite all the negative thoughts in his head (voiced by Gar Private) he manages to remain polite and obedient (mostly) in his public conversations with 'Screwballs'. He does not allow this negativity and insecurity to ruin the relationship they have. Instead, he actually does all the work he is asked to do in the shop (even if he isn't very good at it). By leaving home, he makes the hard decision to try to improve himself and become a better man in later life. Hopefully he succeeds in time to return and enjoy his father's final days. This was a difficult decision but I think it was a good one.

EXAMINER'S ASSESSMENT

There is little reference and no quotation in this answer. Despite this, the candidate does understand the question and has addressed it adequately in broad terms. A focus on a key moment with quotation would improve the overall mark.

MARKS AWARDED

4 + 4 = 8/10 (O2 Grade)

7 The Comparative Study

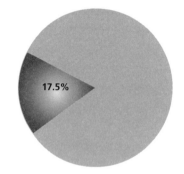

17.5%

- The Comparative Study is worth **70 marks** – this equals 17.5% of the entire exam.
- You should spend about **60–65 minutes** on this section in total.
- Your class will have covered **at least two and maybe even three texts** for this part of the course.
- Every school is different so be **absolutely clear** on **which texts** you have studied.
- You **CANNOT use the 'Single Text'** again in this section.
- These texts can be a **combination** of novels, plays, autobiographies, a film or some other form of text.
- You do **NOT** have to have covered a text by **SHAKESPEARE** – this is compulsory for Higher Level but is **optional for you at Ordinary Level**.
- However, it is very likely that you will have studied a **FILM** – so that becomes an **important part of this section**.

What must I do in the exam?

In simple terms, you must answer a series of questions based upon your texts, under certain headings or 'Modes of Comparison'. They are outlined here:

2020 Exam	–	Hero, Heroine, Villain
		Theme
		Social Setting
2021 Exam	–	Relationships
		Theme
		Social Setting

- **KNOW** the name of your texts and the author/director, etc.
- **READ** these questions very carefully.
- **IDENTIFY** the task in each one.
- **UNDERLINE** the keywords in each one.
- **DECIDE** which mode you will answer on (we will choose 'theme' in the example below).
- **CHOOSE** either number 1 or number 2. Cross out all other questions just to be sure.
- **PLAN** your response:
  - 5 minutes rough work;
  - 12 minutes × 2 for the 15-mark questions;
  - 30 minutes on the 40-mark question;
  - 5 minutes re-reading and correcting at the end.
  - TOTAL TIME = 65 minutes maximum.

Structure of the Comparative Study Section

Use the **3–2–1 formula** for remembering how the Comparative Study section is structured on your exam paper.

- **Three** modes of comparison are prescribed for each year.
- **Two** will appear on the exam paper.
- **One** question – **parts (a) and (b)** – is all that you must do.

Identify which modes are relevant for your year of examination and **thoroughly revise two modes**. This is sufficient to have you prepared for the exam.

Some other points to remember when preparing for this section of the exam:

- You cannot just tell the story of your chosen texts. The purpose of this section is to **test your skills of comparison**.
- This means being able to spot aspects of the texts that are similar. It also involves highlighting differences. You are asked to **compare and contrast** and that is what you are marked on.

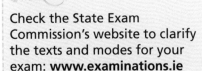

Check the State Exam Commission's website to clarify the texts and modes for your exam: **www.examinations.ie**

Even if you covered three modes in class, revise just **two** of them for the exam.

- The best approach is not to revise all of the material in each text. Instead, focus on a number of **key moments** in each text, which will provide you with the material for exam answers.
- Key moments are often moments of revelation, discovery, choice, tension or climax. Key moments often bring about some kind of change.
- Experience shows that **the same key moments in a text often work with any of the modes.** Be careful in choosing moments or scenes; ensure that they have a major bearing on the story.
- **Be very careful not to confuse the Single Text with the Comparative Texts.** This will lead to automatic disqualification of marks by the examiner.
- At Ordinary Level, you **do not have to study Shakespeare** for the Comparative Study section.

key point

Compare key moments or scenes in your texts. Choose the moments wisely!

Film

The inclusion of film on the Comparative Study section has proven to be very popular. Films can be studied just like any other text, but it is worth noting these points:

- Films **show** you a story; they don't just tell you something. The **theme** of a film is contained in what you see and hear.
- Look carefully at how **colour** is used for effect.
- Be aware of how **sound** and **music** influence your reaction to the story and characters. This includes the soundtrack and the musical score (background or incidental music).
- Films are always located in a certain place and time, a **social setting** with a particular atmosphere.
- Look at how **actors** behave at key moments. How are relationships shaped and developed?
- Films contain great moments of **tension** and **climax**. Know when these occur and remember the resolution (how it all ends).
- Consider from whose **point of view** we see the action unfold. What are we being shown? What or who can we not see?
- What is the main **theme** of the film? All film-makers have something to tell us, which is shown in the work they create. Know exactly what that point is before continuing to revise for your exam. Start by jotting down the main themes of your studied film.

Questions Asked

Two modes will appear on your exam paper. It is likely that you will also have a **choice within the mode**: an A or B option. For example, if you choose to do the **Theme** mode, you will have **two sets of questions** and **you must do one**.

The exam questions are usually split into **two parts**, with the marks divided 30/40:

- The **30-mark question** usually asks about a **mode** of comparison in **one** text.
- The **40-mark question** will require a longer answer. This is where the real business of **comparison with another text (or texts)** takes place.

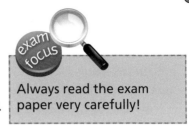

exam focus

Always read the exam paper very carefully!

30-mark questions

The 30-mark questions usually appear as part (a) of a two-part question. You will most likely be asked to write about one text. **You should practise doing short essays (200–300 words) on different modes appearing in one text.**

Recent 30-mark exam questions include the following:

- Name a **theme** from one of your comparative texts. Show how this theme plays an important part in the story.
- Describe **one significant relationship** in one of your chosen texts.
- Choose one of your comparative texts and **outline a relationship that had a strong impact** on you.
- Describe the **social setting** of one of your comparative texts and say whether or not it appealed to you.
- Choose a **person** from one of your texts in your comparative course whose **behaviour you admired or did not admire** and write a short account of him or her.

40-mark questions

The 40-mark questions usually appear as part (b) of a two-part question. **They require you to compare what you have written in (a) to another text you have studied.** You must stick to the question asked and remember your key moments.

Recent 40-mark exam questions include the following:

- Show how the **same theme** was **portrayed differently** in another text from your course.
- Choose a **relationship from another text which was different to the one outlined in (a)**. Say what made this relationship different.
- Choose a **relationship from another text** from your course. Explain **what was different about the impact** this had on you.
- Describe **the social setting of another text** from your comparative studies and show the **similarities and/or differences** that you found when compared to the text in (a). Refer to each text in making your points.
- Choose a **character from another text** from your comparative course. **Compare him or her with the person you have chosen in (a)** and say which of the two you **preferred.**

Preparing for the Exam

The first thing a student must do to revise the Comparative Study is to ask: **which is my favourite text?** Consider the two or three Comparative Texts you have studied (do not include your Single Text) and choose one to use as a base or anchor for your answers. Once you have examined an anchor text and a second text in this way, you have the **raw material for any question** that can appear on your exam paper.

Of all the sections in Paper 2, the Comparative Study section requires the most careful reading of the questions.

Be sure to **include the names** of your **chosen texts and their authors/directors every time** you answer an exam question.

REVISION – all about the 'KEY MOMENTS'

Good exam revision is based around a selection of **key moments** in your text.

Your favourite or **anchor** text is the one you can write about most clearly and confidently in the exam.

- They are typically found at the **start** and the **end** of the text, as well as **turning points, moments of tension** or a 'climax' of some sort.
- Make a list of these for each of your chosen texts. It is likely that **these moments will be central** to any of the questions asked on the paper.

Revise thoroughly **two** of the modes prescribed for the year of your exam.

- **Seven or eight moments** is usually enough for revision purposes.
- These moments – with **quotations** – are what you need to revise.

EXAMPLE – how to manage your revision for Comparative Studies questions

Some texts, such as the novel *The Spinning Heart* or the documentary film *Stop at Nothing: The Lance Armstrong Story* don't exactly follow a traditional 'beginning–middle–end' narrative structure. HOWEVER – the same revision plan applies:

1) FIRST TEXT = *The Spinning Heart* (by Donal Ryan)

The Spinning Heart has an unusual structure which requires careful revision and prioritising certain moments/chapters.

- It is set in an unnamed rural Irish village during **the severe economic crisis** from 2008 onwards that followed the Celtic Tiger years.
- It consists of **21 separate first-person accounts** of how life has panned out for each individual in this **desolate** and **depressing** place.

- A new character is named at the start of each chapter, but the **events do not unfold in a conventional way**, with a beginning, middle and end. Instead, we must piece together the story from all of the fragmented chapters.
- We must rely on the **testimony that these people provide**, sometimes seeming to **contradict** each other and very often **commenting critically upon each other**, in order to understand what has happened.
- The best way to revise this text is to **identify something significant or memorable that each character says**. List these as in the table below.
- You will then find that **some characters** (about six or seven) **seem more significant/central** to the unfolding of the story.
- You will most likely find that the questions and your answers will **focus on these specific characters**.

Character/Chapter	Important Quotations
Bobby (key character #1)	• 'Imagine being a coward and not even knowing it. Imagine being so suddenly useless.' • 'I go there every day to see is he dead and every day he lets me down.'
Josie (key character #2)	• 'Who's to blame when a child turns rotten?' • 'I think of Pokey and I feel disgust, with him and with myself.'
Lily	• 'I love all my children the same way a swallow loves the blue sky; I have no choice in the matter. Like the men that came to my door, nature overpowers me.'
Vasya	• 'I took from others words and phrases that served me well for a while: *off the books, under the table, on the queue tee.*'
Réaltín (key character #3)	• 'There's no one living in any of the other houses, just the ghosts of people who never existed.' • 'I have the whole weekend ahead of me looking forward to Bobby the out-of-work builder coming to trudge around my house.'
Timmy	• 'Bobby was always fair sound to me. He's the only one never slagged me.'
Brian	• 'I won't think about Lorna again once I start tapping some fine blondie wan below in Australia, that's what I'm getting at.'
Trevor	*(A disturbed young man working as a Montessori teacher in the village)* • 'I'm dying. I'm sure of it. One day soon my heart will just stop dead.'

Character/Chapter	Important Quotations
Bridie	• 'How is it at all that I let one child take my whole heart? It wasn't fair on anyone. Life isn't fair, as the fella says.'
Jason	• 'The biggest mistake I made when I was younger was getting tattoos all over my face. The very minute you've a tattoo on your face, the whole world looks at you different.'
Hillary	• 'A lot of those culchies are mad though. They're so *repressed*, like. They all spend their whole lives going to Mass and playing GAA and eating farm animals and cabbage and not saying how they're feeling until it is too late and then BANG! They kill someone. Or themselves.'
Seanie (key character #4)	*(Father to Réaltín's child, a sexual pervert by nature; but also carries deep feelings of depression and loneliness)* • 'I was always a pure solid madman for women. I couldn't stop thinking about them from when I was a small boy.'
Kate	• 'One good thing that happened since the recession started is people will work for less than the minimum wage.'
Lloyd	*(He is an associate of Trevor who conspires in the kidnapping of Réaltín's child from the crèche)* • 'I dreamt I killed the kid. That kind of fucked things up, I can tell you.'
Rory	• 'Every bollocks is going around cribbing about the country being fucked. It'd wear you out, so it would.'
Millicent	• 'Mammy works in Tescos. She told Daddy that she has to work her fingers to the bone. I cried when I heard Mammy say that.'
Denis (key character #5)	*(He actually kills Frank, in a fit of rage one evening, brought on from extreme stress associated with the financial collapse)* • 'I haven't a snowball's chance in hell of a job. I'm owed a small fortune. The sky is falling down.' • 'God help me, I thought I was killing my own father.'
Mags	• 'I just want him to remember how he loved me. I want him to know I'm still his little girl.'
Jim	• 'That was a time when killing was for good, for God and country. That time is long gone.'

Character/Chapter	Important Quotations
Frank (key character #6)	*(Father of Bobby)* ● 'I always had a knack for hitting people where it hurts.' ● 'I could only ever wound a person with my words.' ● "I hadn't time to know I was dying before I was dead. I went quare easy in the end.'
Triona (key character #7)	*(Bobby's wife)* ● 'Bobby hated his father and never got over his mother' ● 'What matters only love?'

By looking at these characters and what they say, certain themes emerge as being common to many of them. The most obvious ones are:

● **Family**

● **Violence**

● **Suffering**

The seven characters highlighted provide the main points for revision. Re-read these chapters before the exam.

But it would also be advisable to remember a quote from each of the 21 characters to further help your answers.

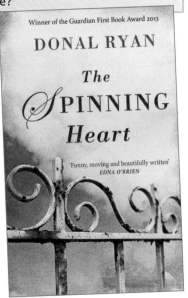

Winner of the Guardian First Book Award 2013

DONAL RYAN

The

*S*PINNING

Heart

'Funny, moving and beautifully written'
EDNA O'BRIEN

2) SECOND TEXT = *Unforgiven* (dir. Clint Eastwood)

The town of **Big Whiskey, Wyoming** is ruled by a sheriff named **Little Bill Daggett** (Gene Hackman). Two cowboys (Davey and Mike) are spending their leave at a brothel owned by **Skinny Dubois**. One of the women, **Delilah**, makes an offhand comment that Mike perceives as an insult, so he attacks her with a knife, scarring her face. The women want Davey and Mike to hang, but Little Bill decides that since they did not murder Delilah, they should be horse-whipped instead. The women pool their resources to offer a reward to anyone who will kill the two attackers.

Enter **William Munny** (Clint Eastwood), a widower and very poor hog farmer, with two young children. He was once a very vicious gunfighter, but after marrying, gave up gun-fighting, drinking and most other vices. Given the desperate situation he and his two children find themselves in, he decides to take up the offer of killing the two cowboys so that he can provide his children with the future that they deserve.

It all leads to a violent conclusion with its unromantic and bleak depiction of life in the Wild West.

Key Moment/Scene	Important Quotations
Opening credits	• (*Note the imagery of sunrise, a lone tree and a grave beside an isolated house*) – 'William Munny, a known thief and murderer, a man of notorious and intemperate disposition.'
Skinny goes to Little Bill	• (*Symbolism: Little Bill is building his house very badly; he's a terrible builder*) – 'they're payin' a thousand dollars to whatever son-of-a-bitch that kills the two boys that cut up Delilah.'
Munny begins to prepare for the mission – he practises shooting	• 'Did Pa used to kill folks?'
Munny and Ned consider what is ahead of them; Munny reflects on his situation	• 'She'd realise I ain't like that no more.' • 'Claudia, she straightened me up, cleared me of drinking whiskey and all. Just cos we're going on this killing don't mean I'm going back to the way I was.' • 'I just need the money; get a new start for them youngsters.'
Little Bill expels English Bob from the town	• 'And tell them there's no whore's gold. And even if there was, well they wouldn't want to come looking for it.'
Munny and Scofield Kid reflect on the reality of killing a man – it's the Kid's first killing and he is emotionally distraught	• 'I killed the hell outta him, didn't I; three shots and he was taking a shit'. • 'Take a drink, Kid' • 'It's a hell of a thing killing a man; you take away all he's got, and all he's ever gonna have.' • 'I guess he had it coming.' • 'We all have it coming, Kid'
Shoot-out in Greeley's 'Shithole' Saloon – the violent showdown	• 'Well, you be William Munny from out Missouri, killer of women and children.' • 'And I'm here to kill you Little Bill, for what you did to Ned.' • 'Deserve's got nothing to do with it.' • 'I'll see you in Hell, William Munny.'

Putting answers together

By re-reading/re-watching these key moments (suggested by the texts above) and memorising the quotations, it then becomes possible to answer questions on one or other of the MODES on the day.

- Break your own texts down in this fashion.
- Perhaps this is what your teacher has done already.
- The same approach is useful, no matter what text you have studied.

Third text?

If your teacher has studied a **third text** during fifth or sixth year, then once again fill out the key moments in your own words. Use the box below as a guide.

Text = ...

Key Moments	Quotations

> **IMPORTANT!**
> Exam answers sometimes ask that you refer to 'at least two texts.' This means that **TWO IS ENOUGH.**
> Choose the **two that you enjoyed the most** and answer the questions based upon them.

Answering exam questions

Of the three **modes** each year, two will appear on your exam paper. **theme** is a mode that is prescribed for both 2020 and 2021. It also appeared on the 2019 exam paper.

Read the following questions on **theme** taken from the 2019 examination. Then look closely at the sample answer that follows.

SECTION II THE COMPARATIVE STUDY (70 MARKS), 2019 EXAM

Candidates must answer ONE question from either A – Relationships, or B – Theme. In your answer you may not use the text you have answered on in SECTION I – The Single Text. All texts used in this section must be prescribed for comparative study for this year's examination. Candidates may refer to only one film in the course of their answers. N.B. The questions use the word text to refer to all the different kinds of texts available for study on this course, i.e. novel, play, short story, autobiography, biography, travel writing and film.

B – THEME

1.   (a) (i) Identify a theme you explored in **one** of the three comparative texts you have studied, and select a character who reveals something important to you about your chosen theme. Explain the way(s) in which your chosen character reveals something important about your chosen theme to you.   **(15)**

(ii) Choose a character from **another** comparative text you have studied and, with reference to the same theme you discussed in part (i), explain the way(s) in which your chosen character reveals something important about your chosen theme to you. **(15)**

(b) 'We can find a theme to be more realistic and true-to-life in some texts than in others.'

In relation to the theme you discussed in part (a) above, compare how realistic and true-to-life you found this theme to be in **at least two** texts on your comparative course. Support your answer with reference to your chosen texts. **(40)**

Answering the Comparative Study question

To answer this question, we will choose the theme of **FAMILY**. We will refer to Josie Burke from *The Spinning Heart* for the first question, then William Munny from *Unforgiven* for the second question. Then for the 40-mark question, we will consider which of the two texts presents a more realistic picture of family.

SAMPLE ANSWER

1. (a) (i)   The most interesting character to illustrate the theme was **Josie Burke, Pokey's father.** Josie's chapter is the second in the book and he fills in many important plot details. He admits, more or less, that he is a failure as a father, loving his children unequally and treating his wife poorly. He then observes that the decision to sell off the Cunliffe family land was the start of the major problems in the village. Nothing good comes from this decision. Josie admits in hindsight: **'We should have known it would all end in tears. Around here, it all started with tears.'** The division of the land like **'our Lord's purple robe'** and removing the Cunliffe **'family name'** serves as a curse on the village, sending many people's hearts 'spinning' and their worlds toppling. Josie feels disgust, **'with him and with myself'**, referring to the way he raised Pokey to be so greedy and selfish. He feels very guilty over what has ultimately happened in the village.

The breakdown of family values, decency and respect for tradition, which causes 'dysfunction' in the village, is the theme that dominates the book and Josie Burke is wise enough and old enough to realise this in his chapter.

(204 words)

EXAMINER'S ASSESSMENT

This is an excellent answer as it includes each of the required components: text, author, theme, character and each significant point is backed up with quotations and supporting comments. This deserves top marks.

MARKS AWARDED

9 + 6 = 15/15 (O1 Grade)

(ii) **William Munny** from *Unforgiven* is a widower, a hog farmer and father of two children; he becomes the hero of the film, although he does engage in the ruthless killing of a number of others to achieve his goal. From early in the film, we see that Munny is trying to live a different life to that of his former years as a gunslinger and *'a man of notoriously vicious and intemperate disposition'*. He pledged to his departed wife Claudia, before she died from smallpox, that he would give the children the life that they deserve and he does his best to succeed as both farmer and father. Unfortunately, in 1880 he and the children are in dire poverty and the hogs are sick. It forces him to take on his role as a ruthless killer one last time. The film strongly hints that a father like Munny will do absolutely anything to ensure his children succeed. It also shows that Munny is quite disturbed by this challenge. He says to his partner Ned: *'I ain't like that no more.'* Despite this, he completes his mission by killing Little Bill Daggett, collects his money and returns to his children. For him, *'it's a hell of a thing killing a man.'* But honouring his dead wife and doing everything necessary for their children, even killing other men, is the most important thing in life. Family is everything to him.

(238 words)

EXAMINER'S ASSESSMENT

A very good answer, addressing the theme of family. Lots of plot details here and three quotations are used. Vocabulary is of a very good standard too.

MARKS AWARDED

9 + 6 = 15/15 (O1 Grade)

(NOTE – comparative language/examples are underlined in the answer to part (b))

1. (b) Both *The Spinning Heart* and *Unforgiven* contain scenes where family issues are evident. It is difficult to say if the storylines are realistic or if one is more realistic than the other. But I would conclude that *The Spinning Heart* is so full of family misery and problems that such a village could not possibly exist in the real world. There seems to be almost no happiness in any of its chapters.

On the other hand, despite the violence and harshness of the movie *Unforgiven*, I think it is a slightly more realistic story than what *The Spinning Heart* shows us. It highlights the genuine hardships that families faced in America at this time, when people had to do desperate things to survive.

Unlike Josie Burke, who comes across as powerless to do anything about the fall of his family's reputation, William Munny is determined to ensure his children don't follow his bad habits or wicked ways. He is also doing it to honour the memory of their mother Claudia: *'I just need the money; get a new start for them youngsters.'* This is different to Josie who despite working hard himself, effectively admits that he is responsible for making a mess of rearing his two sons: *'Who's to blame when a child turns rotten?'* He sounds like he has given up on his sons ever turning things around.

However, Munny's determination is a more realistic image of what fathers and mothers do in order to see their children thrive. He doesn't give up on them. His violent actions may seem immoral, but there is a sense of justice behind them. He eliminates the corrupt sheriff and his deputies, avenges the awful crimes suffered by Delilah and Ned, and collects his reward with which to support his children in the future.

He is also very realistic and blunt about what he has to do in the most famous scene of the film. When Scofield Kid emotionally breaks down after killing one of the cowboys, Munny remarks: *'It's a hell of a thing killing a man; you take away all he's got, and all he's ever gonna have.'* He also notes that death is coming everybody's way eventually: *'We all have it coming, Kid.'* This is in contrast to so many of the characters in *The Spinning Heart* who speak about their family problems but don't appear to have any solutions. Bobby's wife Triona memorably asks *'What matters only love?'* It is a pity that the characters don't take her words seriously as *The Spinning Heart* is a book where every family seems to be dysfunctional and broken. If they had to live in Big

Whiskey in 1880, they would know what real hardship was all about.

Therefore, while both books contain extreme examples of family hardship, *Unforgiven*, for all its violence, is slightly more realistic in my opinion.

(480 words)

EXAMINER'S ASSESSMENT

An interesting and thought-provoking response. The question invites a number of possible answers – the candidate makes a choice and argues using example, quotation and includes comparative language. This indicates a wide knowledge of both the storyline and the themes in the texts. A top-scoring effort.

MARKS AWARDED

12 + 12 + 12 + 4 = 40/40 (O1 Grade)

Useful Phrases

There are certain words and phrases that are useful for the Comparative Study. Examiners are on the lookout for them. Provided they are accurate and relevant, you stand a greater chance of scoring well in this section if you include certain phrases. Try to incorporate the following phrases into your answers.

When looking for similarities:

- 'In both texts ...'
- 'Similarly to text A, text B ...'
- 'I also noted/found/saw/felt that ...'
- 'This also occurs/happens/exists in ...'
- 'When we look at text B ...'
- 'Text A and B both show/demonstrate/indicate/portray ...'
- 'In the same way ...'
- 'Once again, we see that ...'

When looking for differences:

- 'In contrast ...'
- 'Unlike in text A ...'
- 'What a difference from ...'
- 'This is the reverse of ...'
- 'This is the opposite to ...'
- 'I found that text B differs ...'
- 'While X happens in text A, Y happens in text B ...'

Essential words and phrases:

- Unlike
- Like
- Similar
- Different
- Contrastingly
- Too
- Also
- Yet

- But
- Whereas
- On the other hand
- However
- Nevertheless
- Consequently
- As a result
- Therefore

8 Poetry

There are two poetry sections in the exam:

a) Unseen Poem (20 marks/20 minutes)

b) Studied Poetry (50 marks/45 minutes)

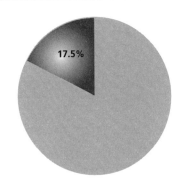

17.5%

The Vocabulary of Poetry – 'Poetic Terms'

Poetry has a language and style of its own. It is different to other types of writing. Therefore, it is important to be familiar with some terms or techniques that are associated with poetry. Being really familiar with the list on the next page can help improve your written responses. Good answers often include reference to one or other of these terms.

Eavan Boland

Robert Frost

Sylvia Plath

D. H. Lawrence

The 12 Most Important Poetic Terms!

ALLITERATION: A technique where (usually) the same letter is used repeatedly at the beginning of words in close succession.

E.g.: *'long, lovely and lush'* (Hopkins in 'Spring') makes the grass seem like it is shooting upwards.

ASSONANCE: The use of similar sounding vowel sounds in poetry, they create a particular sound effect.

E.g.: *'The sty was plastered halfway up with glass-smooth dung'* from Elizabeth Bishop's poem 'The Prodigal'.

IMAGERY: This is the creation of pictures in the mind of the reader that can have an effect upon the reader's feelings, understandings or reactions. All poetry contains some imagery.

E.g.: *'a dirty dog, quite comfy'* (Bishop in 'Filling Station') is a wonderful picture to imagine on a hot day in rural America.

METAPHOR: A word or phrase to describe something which must not be understood literally. Much poetry is metaphoric because poets aim to describe things in colourful, abstract ways.

E.g.: *'our broken images rebuild/Themselves around your limbs'* (Boland in 'Child of Our Time') is a particularly powerful image.

ONOMATOPOEIA: This involves words which imitate sounds, or where the sound matches closely with the intended meaning.

E.g.: *'rollrock highroad roaring down'* (Hopkins in 'Inversnaid') brilliantly captures the sound and movement of a waterfall.

PERSONIFICATION: This is to give human characteristics to non-human subjects, or to give life, metaphorically, to sometimes lifeless things.

E.g.: *'They stuck out their little feet and snored'* gives human characteristics to the pigs in Elizabeth Bishop's 'The Prodigal'.

PUN: A play on words, which creates a double meaning, sometimes, but not always, for comic effect.

E.g.: *'The boy saw all'* (Frost in 'Out, Out—') suggests the boy now understands the real danger he is in, having actually cut his hand with a saw.

SIMILE: This is a description that uses 'as', 'like' or sometimes 'than', to make a comparison between two related subjects. The things being compared may not have an obvious likeness.

E.g.: *'And then he flew as far as eye could see'* is a very simple and clear example of simile in Robert Frost's 'The Tuft of Flowers'.

SPEAKER: The **voice** in the poem. **The poet is NOT always the one speaking in the poem,** though often they are the same. 'La Belle Dame Sans Merci' by John Keats is a good example of where more than one voice in the poem is heard and where the voice is not always that of the poet.

STANZA: This is the correct term for a **collection of lines together** in a poem. **Sonnets** have fourteen lines, but can be broken into various 'stanzas' or specific groups of lines. It is a good idea to use this word 'stanza' when answering questions.

THEME: The main idea or issue discussed in a poem. It is not necessarily the subject-matter, but rather the **deeper concern** or **message** that is raised or discussed in the poem.

> E.g.: **Mystery** is a key theme in Eiléan Ní Chuilleanáin's poem 'Street', even though it describes the movements of a woman working in a butchers.

TONE: Associated with feeling or mood, one can imagine the tone of the poem being the sound of the voice that speaks in the poem. It creates a certain mood or 'feeling' to the words.

> E.g.: **Anxiety** and **despair** are the dominant tones in 'Child' by Sylvia Plath.

Answering Questions – Part 1: The Unseen Poem

Unseen Poem (20 MARKS/20 MINUTES)

- The unseen poem is not too complicated. You will be asked for a reaction to specific issues after some **careful reading**.
- Its purpose is to **test your response to poetry generally** before tackling specific prescribed poetry.
- There are usually **two short questions** asked, both worth 10 marks. There may be a 20-mark question on its own.
- Answers worth 10 marks require about **100 words**. This is about six or seven full sentences as a minimum.
- Answers worth 20 marks require at least two full paragraphs, **up to about 200 words or more**.
- Stick to the '**point–quote–explain**' formula: say something at first, refer and quote from the poem, and explain what you mean.
- It is important to '**move on**' from this question after fifteen minutes. More questions worth more marks are waiting.

Typical questions include:

- **Feelings** generated in the poem;
- **Images** and settings created in the poem;
- **Sounds** heard in the language of the poem;
- **Themes** in the poem: what is the main point being made?
- Your **reaction** to the poem – did you like it? etc.

NOTE: This final point – 'your reaction' – can be a challenging question for 20 marks/15 minutes of work.

If asked for 'your reaction' to the Unseen Poem, refer back to the 'poetic techniques' above:

- Write down what **you** noticed or felt having read the poem.
- Refer to major features like **imagery** or the **theme** of the poem.
- Top-grade answers often explain how the poem makes you 'feel' having read it.
- You are likely to cover some important aspects of the poem in your answer if you follow this advice.

Students that can identify feelings or emotions in the written word typically score well in their answers.

Sample Question 1 – Unseen Poem (20 marks/20 minutes)

Read this poem at least twice and then respond to the questions that follow.

The Scottish poet, Douglas Dunn, writes a poem in which he explores his feelings about a family leaving their home in the city.

A REMOVAL FROM TERRY STREET

On a squeaking cart, they push the usual stuff,
A mattress, bed ends, cups, carpets, chairs,
Four paperback westerns. Two whistling youths
In surplus US Army battle-jackets
Remove their sister's goods. Her husband
Follows, carrying on his shoulders the son
Whose mischief we are glad to see removed,
And pushing, of all things, a lawnmower.
There is no grass in Terry Street. The worms
Come up cracks in concrete yards in moonlight.
That man, I wish him well. I wish him grass.

Douglas Dunn

1. What kind of world is being described in this poem? Refer to the poem in your answer. **(10)**
2. How, in your opinion, does the writer feel about the family that is leaving Terry Street? Refer to the text of the poem in your answer. **(10)**

QUESTION 1
SAMPLE ANSWER

The world of this poem is an urban one, where poverty is apparent. The fact that 'there is no grass on Terry Street' tells me that this must be in a town or city and the poet seems to be laughing at the fact that the family have a lawnmower. The brothers are wearing 'surplus US Army battle-jackets' and pushing a cart with all the family belongings. They are not moving house but instead are being 'removed', as the title says. I think that this may be because they cannot afford the rent or are being re-housed because of anti-social behaviour, perhaps caused by the son who sits on the father's shoulders.

(114 words)

EXAMINER'S ASSESSMENT

This is a really good answer for ten marks. It makes an excellent opening claim that is well supported with five pieces of evidence. The reference to the title is apt and shows that the candidate has read the poem closely.

MARKS AWARDED

6 + 4 = 10/10

QUESTION 2
SAMPLE ANSWER

I think that the poet has some sympathy for the family. It is contained mostly in the final line. When he says 'I wish him well', I feel that he understands the shame and hardship that is felt if you are thrown out of your house. He sees that the man is doing his best for his family, having a lawnmower that might be used if they get a good new house or make some money if he sells it. He is glad that the son is going, 'whose mischief we are glad to see going', but overall, he does feel a bit sorry for them.

(107 words)

EXAMINER'S ASSESSMENT

This is a really good answer that includes the key word 'sympathy' in the opening sentence. Two quotations are included to back up the claim and the candidate addresses the question with a broad and carefully chosen vocabulary.

MARKS AWARDED

6 + 4 = 10/10
Total for Unseen Poem = 20/20 (O1 Grade)

Sample Question 2 – Unseen Poem (20 marks/20 minutes).

Read the following poem and the two questions on it at least twice before writing your answers.

SEAGULL

We are the dawn marauders.*
We prey on pizza. We kill kebabs.
We mug thrushes for bread crusts
with a snap of our big bent beaks.
We drum the worms from the ground
with the stamp of our wide webbed feet.
We spread out, cover the area –
like cops looking for the body
of a murdered fish-supper.
Here we go with our hooligan yells
loud with gluttony, sharp with starvation.
Here we go bungee-jumping on the wind,
charging from the cold sea of our birth.
This is invasion. This is occupation.
Our flags are black, white and grey.
Our wing-stripes are our rank.
No sun can match the brazen
colour of our mad yellow eyes.

We are the seagulls.
We are the people.

Brian McCabe
*(raiders/robbers)

1. In this poem the poet vividly describes the actions and conduct of seagulls. Choose two of these descriptions which appeal to you most. Explain your choices. **(10)**

2. *We are the seagulls.*
   We are the people.

   From your reading of the poem, what similarities do you think the poet draws between seagulls and humans? Explain your answer. **(10)**

QUESTION 1
SAMPLE ANSWER

I like when he says that the seagulls are like cops looking for a body and when they have mad yellow eyes. The cops are the police so I think he means that the seagulls are like them. People don't like the cops and sometimes seagulls are not liked either. Maybe it's just that they have to do a job when they need to find food they have to kill other animals. Their eyes are mad and yellow and this makes them seem fierce and wicked birds. Overall, it is a really vivid description.

(95 words)

EXAMINER'S ASSESSMENT

The candidate engages with the task and does answer the question asked. Two examples are selected but the candidate would score better with more accurate quotation or by making two distinct points. A 'personal' interpretation of the scene is provided. The language and expression is quite basic but this merits half marks for the effort made.

MARKS AWARDED

3 + 2 = 5/10

QUESTION 2
SAMPLE ANSWER

The seagulls are very like humans the way they kill things and cause trouble for others. 'Here we go with our hooligan yells' is like the way mad football fans riot and cause fights all over the place. I didn't think hooligans were like birds, they are more like wild animals when they get going. I seen many hooligan on the telly but none of them looked like seagulls. But then again, the birds here are described like people so maybe next time I see a seagull, I will think of them as vicious birds that cause trouble for other creatures around them, just like hooligans do.

(108 words)

EXAMINER'S ASSESSMENT

This is an excellent example of a candidate with limited skills really trying to say as much as they can to earn marks. **Crucially, the basic question is answered**: birds are equated with hooligans and the candidate expands upon that idea, with reference to the poem and some personal input. Well done.

MARKS AWARDED

5 + 2 = 7/10

Total = 12/20 (O4 Grade)

key point

You are not asked to 'explain everything' in the unseen poem, but rather to say what the poem means to you.

Answering Questions – Part 2: Prescribed Poetry (50 Marks/45 minutes)

- Spend about five minutes reading the options and highlighting key words.
- Spend 25 minutes answering the short 10-mark questions and 15 minutes on the longer 20-mark question.
- Total = 45 minutes.
- **Four poems** from your full list will appear on the page.
- Each year, the exam papers have shown that **two** poems come from a combined list studied by everybody doing the exam – Higher or Ordinary Level.
- **Two** more poems come from a list confined to just Ordinary Level.
- It is important to concentrate on **one list only**.
- **There is no need to revise every poem on the course.**
- This is particularly true if you have been in a class with **mixed Higher/Ordinary** Level students.
- In this book, we will focus on revising just the poems that are found on the combined **Higher/Ordinary** list as most students will have covered these poems.

Choose your poems for revision – don't try to revise them all! Just look at the lists below – you will end up revising about twenty at the very most.

2020 & 2021	
E. Boland:	'Child of Our Time'
	'This Moment'
	'Love'
P. Durcan:	'Wife Who Smashed Television Gets Jail'
	'Parents'
	'Sport'
R. Frost:	'The Tuft of Flowers'
	'Out, Out—'

2020 only	
E. Dickinson:	'I felt a Funeral, in my Brain'
	'I heard a Fly buzz–when I died'
D. H. Lawrence:	'Humming-Bird'
	'Baby-Movements II, "Trailing Clouds"'
E. Ní Chuilleanáin:	'Street'
	'To Niall Woods and Xenya Ostrovskaia, married in Dublin on 9 September 2009'
A. Rich:	'Aunt Jennifer's Tigers'
	'Uncle Speaks in the Drawing Room'

2020 only	
W. Wordsworth:	'She dwelt among the untrodden ways'
	'It is a beauteous evening, calm and free'
	from *The Prelude*: 'Skating'
R. Frost:	'Mending Wall'

2021 only	
E. Bishop:	'The Fish'
	'The Prodigal'
	'Filling Station'
S. Heaney:	'A Constable Calls'
	'The Underground'
	'A Call'
G. M. Hopkins:	'Spring'
	'Inversnaid'
J. Keats:	'On First Looking into Chapman's Homer'
	'La Belle Dame Sans Merci'
S. Plath:	'Poppies in July'
	'Child'

How do I revise my prescribed poetry?

Use the SEE–HEAR–FEEL approach to revision

People are instinctively drawn to one of three main reactions to a piece of writing. We are mostly:

1. LOOKERS (visual learners)

OR

2. HEARERS (audio learners)

OR

3. FEELERS (emotional learners)

Of course, we all have eyes, ears and emotions. The point is that we sometimes have **one which is stronger than the other two,** often without realising it. Applied to poetry, this means:

- **Looker**: Yes, I can see the **imagery** of the poem, the colours and shapes, the faces of the people, and the location/ setting is clear.

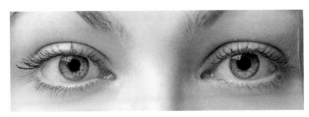

- **Hearer**: Yes, I can hear the beat and rhythm of this poem. I can appreciate the **language** usage. The words sound good to me and I like the way it rhymes (if it does) or the way the poet brings music to the scene.

- **Feeler**: Yes, the poem affected the way I felt. I could feel a certain **tone** – it created a certain mood. It made an impact upon me and I could relate to the experience of the speaker/poet. There was a strong emotional impact within it.

When you put all three together, you should have a sense of what the point of the poem is. You will hopefully grasp the **theme** of the poem.

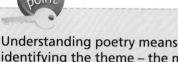

key point

Understanding poetry means identifying the theme – the main issue within – once you have considered the imagery, language and tone.

Question 1: 30 Marks/25 Minutes

Question 1, parts **a**, **b** and **c**, each worth 10 marks, look for specifics from within the poem. Typical questions asked recently include:

- Specific issues: **content/tone/imagery, etc.**
- **How** does the poet create **image/atmosphere/setting?**
- What do we **learn** from this poem?
- What is your **favourite phrase/line** in the poem?
- Why do you think this poem is so **popular?**
- What **questions are raised** by this poem?
- How would you **feel** if you were ... etc.?
- What is the **message** of the poem?
- Describe the **relationship** between ... etc.

Have a look at the notes on this prescribed poem and the typical approach to a 10-mark question.

Notes on Prescribed Poems

1. Gerard Manley Hopkins (2021) 'Spring'

See	Hear	Feel
Springtime; weeds, wheels, bird's eggs; woodland coming 'alive' and lambs running in the fields; speaker wonders **what causes all this to happen?** remembers the 'Garden of Eden' in the Bible; **a time before sin,** when we were innocent, just like the animals in the fields. **Powerful religious imagery** throughout, calling us to prayer and repentance.	Wonderful **sounds** throughout this poem, e.g. **assonance** – weeds and wheels; **alliteration** – long, lovely, low, look, little, low; birdsong – 'echoing timber'; rinse and wring'; 'strikes like lightnings'; lambs playing – 'have fair their fling'; **wonder** at this beautiful scene – 'all this juice and joy'.	**Awe** and **amazement** – spring is such an **awe-inspiring** time; the re-awakening of the earth and the **joy of life** itself; the last six lines pose a question: **how can we retain all this wonder and joy before sin clouds our minds?** Speaker feels that it is **Christ that saves us from sin.**

Typical 10-mark question and answer

- This poem appeared on the 2017 exam paper as well as in 2011. Here is an example of a 10-mark question and sample answer to go with it.
- Look at how the grid above – 'see–hear–feel' – can help with answering these types of questions.
- Remember that for 10 marks, you should write at least six or seven sentences in about 8–10 minutes.
- As always: point–quote–explain.

Question

Do you think Hopkins creates a sense of prayer in the last six lines of the poem? Refer to the poem in support of your answer. (10 marks)

SAMPLE ANSWER

I **agree** that Hopkins **creates a sense of prayer** in the last six lines. This is because the **imagery is mostly religious,** or at least in my mind, it makes me think of **religious themes. (Point)**

Words like **'Christ, lord'** and the mention of **'Maid's child'** indicate the person of Jesus. There is also a mention of the **Garden of Eden**. These images recall our fall from grace and how humans became sinful. **(Quote/Reference)**

This poem therefore is a celebration of all that is beautiful in nature, especially in spring. But we also must pray for our sinfulness in this beautiful world because according to Hopkins, it is 'worth the winning' when Christ saves us. **(Explain)**

(113 words)

EXAMINER'S ASSESSMENT

This answer would receive the full 10 marks as it does exactly what is required from the question.

Now apply the same type of approach with the rest of the poems and notes below.

'Inversnaid'

See	Hear	Feel
Speaker finds himself alongside a **small Scottish stream** – a 'darksome burn, horseback brown' that roars down the hillside; froth and bubbles; dark pools; it rolls through steep hillsides (braes) and through boggy ground (heathpack, fern); speaker wonders aloud **what the world would be like without this wet and wild scenery?**	The **power of the river**: darksome, horseback, rollrock, highroad, coop, comb, fleece, foam, flutes, lake falls home; 'fawn-froth' suggests **the slower movement further down**; there is **alliteration** all throughout: 'degged – dappled – dew'; 'flitches of fern'; 'Long live the weeds and the wilderness yet'; **suggests the stream is ongoing, like life itself.**	**Awe** in the face of such raw power and beauty; speaker is **enthralled** by this apparently minor little stream flowing down the hillside; speaker turns to **wonder** what the world would be like without ('bereft of') this wild and beautiful scene; **defiant** at the end, **hoping that this scene will continue forever.**

2. Eiléan Ní Chuilleanáin (2020)
'Street'

See	Hear	Feel
A mysterious scene, unexplained; an unnamed man sees a butcher's daughter; **mesmerised** by her beauty, seeing her white trousers and dangling knife; **follows her** down a laneway; a half-open door, stairs with her **bloody footprints** leading to the top; **what is about to happen and why?** We don't know.	A simple **narrative poem** – it tells a **story**; the verb **'dangling'** is important – the detail is left out there for us; we do not know what is going on or what will happen next; **'shambles'** is an old word for the **'slaughterhouse'**, but also a **'mess'** or a **'confusion'**: We **watch rather than listen** to this scene.	A slightly **'sinister'** poem – maybe an **innocent fantasy** of a young man; but the specific details – butcher, knife, love, laneway, door, bloodstains, bare feet – are the **typical details of a murder mystery** or a gothic horror scene; something **uncomfortable** and **odd** about these unexplained events.

'To Niall Woods and Xenya Ostrovskaia, Married in Dublin On 9th September 2009'

See	Hear	Feel
A newly married couple, setting out on a journey, the **metaphor** of 'following a star'; given a **'mother's blessing'**; arriving in a new land, discovering new things but remembering those from the past; part of a 'fairytale'; **things will work out in the end, according to the mother**; just like Ruth, the Moabite woman in the Old Testament.	'Pitching its tent' – a **metaphor** for settling down together; **'You will'** is repeated – the mother is certain about the future; the 'talking cat' is an **image** from folklore, associated with witches, or the **'wise old woman'**; 'trust' is a key word – the speaker asks that they **trust in her wisdom and her blessing**.	**Mild humour** throughout; a **quirky** and **unusual** 'mother's blessing' to a newly married couple; she speaks with wisdom: 'leave behind', you will find, 'you will see', 'you will have to trust me'. The end is **uplifting**: for all the uncertainty about the future and the troubles she faced, things worked out fine for Ruth in the Bible.

3. Eavan Boland (2020 and 2021)
'Child of Our Time'

See	Hear	Feel
Child being sung to sleep – a 'lullaby' – changes to a **death scene**; baby screaming; **contrasts dramatically** with the gentle, homely imagery of a baby at rest, in bed; **adults wondering** how to react – 'idle talk' has led to the death; cradle has been 'robbed'; baby is now 'asleep' in death; **we must not let this happen again.**	References to **music** contrasts with the subject of a bomb exploding: **'lullaby; song; cry; tune; rhythm; rhymes'**; harsh, blunt language describes the dead child – **'discord; murder; death; dead; broken'**. Numerous **emotive phrases** – 'the discord of your murder', 'robbed your cradle' we 'hear' the **cries of pain and anguish**.	**Tenderness** and **love** are evident at the beginning; but this is destroyed by the sense of **outrage** and **anguish** in stanza 2 – adults 'should have known how' to avoid this needless killing; there is some **hope** in the end – maybe from this death we can 'rebuild' ourselves around this image, to **ensure it won't happen again.**

'This Moment'

See	Hear	Feel
Somewhere in the **'suburbs'** – evening time – and we are **peering in the window of a family home**; stars and moths in the sky; black dark contrasts with the yellow colours inside; a child runs to its mother's arms; **everything happens very quickly** – then the 'moment' passes.	**'Neighbourhood'** suggests a community of neighbours, **friendly and in conversation**; but there is a **'silence'** about this moment; it will also pass very quickly; 'yellow as butter' is a **simile**; even in such silence, many things are happening; perhaps **we don't pay enough attention to these small things?**	**Anticipation** – 'things are getting ready/to happen/out of sight'; **mystery** – what is actually going on? The arrival of darkness makes us **slightly fearful**; but the comforting arms of the mother **reassures us**; 'apples sweeten' suggests a pleasant ending; but fruit can **metaphorically suggest** the loss of innocence.

'Love'

See	Hear	Feel
Speaker addresses her husband; remembering life in midwest America; **river represents the journey of their love together**; remembering their challenges, how **love was fragile**: 'feather and muscle of wings'; 'fire and air'; how their child nearly died; now **they are older**, the speaker sees the husband as a hero; but wonders **will their love ever be so intense again**?	Bridge, river, water – all suggest **a journey or a challenge ahead**; references to 'hero' evoke myths and legends – their journey together has been difficult and not without troubles; 'Amish' reference makes it seem very **basic, unexciting**; now 'we speak plainly' and 'we hear each other clearly' suggest that **both are now wiser and more understanding**.	**Sombre, serious** tone at the beginning – **remembering the past** but in a 'matter-of-fact' way; **calm, reflective** tones in stanzas 2–4; changes in stanza 5 to a **longing for a return** to more 'romantic' times – 'blazing', 'gilded' and 'epic' call for a more intense, exciting relationship; a **sense of uncertainty** at the end – never the same again?

4. Paul Durcan (2020 and 2021)
'Wife Who Smashed Television Gets Jail'

See	Hear	Feel
Courtroom scene, but something **comical** about it all; lines 1–21: the 'evidence' of the husband; lots of **ludicrous details**, e.g. 'took off her boots and smashed in the television'; 'mother has a fondness for *Kojak*'; lines 22–26: the **Judge pronounces his verdict** – again with ludicrous detail: 'television... a basic unit of the family'; 'leave to appeal was refused.'	**Ranting, agitated husband** and father delivering his evidence; attempts to be formal: 'My Lord'; **violent actions are indicated:** 'smashed; marched; boot through the screen; snarled;' the judgement is delivered in **formal tones but with a comical edge** – 'Jail is the only place for them'.	**Disturbing** detail on the surface; this is a reversal of the more likely scene – it is **discomforting** to have a mother, rather than a father, doing this to her family; a **strange mix between tragedy and comedy** – a sense of drama and conflict mixed with the **bizarre details of the case**; ultimately, a **comical poem, poking fun** at the sensitive topic of domestic violence.

'Parents'

See	Hear	Feel
A child's face – the word '**drowned**' and the repetition of '**sea**' makes this a **frightening image**; metaphorically, the child is '**in danger**'; 'locked out of their own home' suggests a **distance or a great danger in the parent–child relationship**; 'fearful fish' and 'calling out to them' continue the **frightening imagery**; parents left '**stranded**', staring at their 'lost child'.	'**Sea**' and '**See**' (pun) are both used – the 'sea' of sleep? or the 'sea' of confusion? 'locked out' – a very **harsh sounding phrase**; child calling out in the night; **parents cannot hear nor respond**; a very **distressing sound**; 'inside' versus 'outside' and repetition of 'drowned' suggests **the sound of panic and desperation** on the part of the parents.	**Distressing** and **disturbing**; a sense of **distance and disconnection between parents and child**; 'mouths open' create the sense that the parents are in **shock** or in **panic**; 'they cannot hear'; 'they are outside the sea'; 'they stare at the drowned, drowned face'; a **genuinely downbeat and 'depressing' tone throughout**.

'Sport'

See	Hear	Feel
Father hoping the son will succeed at sport; son is in a **psychiatric hospital** but plays a game of football, as **goalkeeper**; father spectates; various **vulnerable and disturbed characters play on the team**; son plays really well: 'I did not flinch in the goals'; son had **tried incredibly hard to please the father**; he never managed to do so again after this event.	**Narrative language** – 'I was selected to play for Grangegorman Mental Hospital'; very **colourful and varied characters** play on both teams – 'gapped teeth, red faces, oily frizzy hair, bushy eyebrows ... cases of schizophrenia'; **father finally praises his son** as he sniffs his approval: '**Well played, son**'.	**Reflective** – speaker remembers the '**one time**' father praised him; **fearful** that he would 'let him down'; **pride** that he played so well; **mixed feelings now** on reflection – he seldom if ever rose to these heights again.

5. Robert Frost (2020 and 2021)
'The Tuft of Flowers'

See	Hear	Feel
Rural or 'pastoral' scene, speaker is **alone**, ready to turn the freshly mown grass; **mysterious 'other' figure** cut it yesterday; butterfly also notices the scene; a small tuft remains uncut amid the mown grass; the speaker feels a 'spirit kindred' with the other worker, who 'spared' this tuft; **they share the same views and opinions, even though they don't know each other**.	**Beautifully crafted phrases**: 'isle of trees'; 'whetstone' (used to sharpen the blade); 'bewildered butterfly'; 'tremulous wing'; 'tall tuft of flowers'; 'leaping tongue of bloom'; 'reedy brook'; 'the scythe had spared'; 'I worked no more alone'; 'held brotherly speech'; 'Men work together'.	**Loneliness**; lacking any enthusiasm; changes to **delight** when the butterfly shows him the tuft of flowers; **spirit is uplifted** with this 'message from the dawn'; **relaxed and contented** at the end – the flowers are a **sign of life and the presence of another**, similar-minded person.

'Mending Wall' (2020)

See	Hear	Feel
Rural scene; a wall is being repaired by the speaker and his neighbour; they speak to each other; **it is like a game, but not quite friendly**; it seems quite **normal and routine**, but holding the stones, the neighbour looks like a 'savage'; they agree that '**good fences make good neighbours**'.	'Frozen-ground-swell': some **invisible force makes the wall fall down**; 'we meet to walk the line'; 'we wear our fingers rough'; 'Why do they make good neighbours?'; the neighbour 'moves in darkness as it seems to me'; 'walling in or walling out?'; 'Like an old stone savage armed'; **lots of questioning phrases**.	**Friendly banter**; sense of 'purpose' and good relationships; leads to **curiosity and uncertainty**; speaker is **not entirely pleased** – why the need for walls? Why not live and let live? Speaker **accepts that the neighbour will not change** – the wall will remain; life goes on as before.

'Out, Out—' (2020 and 2021)

See	Hear	Feel
Rural Vermont; young boy working hard sawing timber; evening time; work nearly done; **boy cuts his hand very badly;** panic; sister is with him; doctor tries to save him but **it's too late; he dies;** the other people don't seem too bothered; **life 'carries on'** as they 'turned to their affairs'.	**Sharp, clear sounds** of the work being done: 'buzz-saw' 'snarled and rattled'; 'stove-length sticks of wood'; 'sunset'; 'supper'; 'But the hand!'; 'a rueful laugh'; **'the boy saw all'** – a great **pun**; 'big boy doing a man's work'; 'the watcher at his pulse took fright'; 'little–less–nothing' and **'they'** don't seem to care too much.	**Pride** – 'hard work' is what makes a boy into a man; **anticipation** of supper; replaced by **shock** – the saw 'leaped out of the boy's hand'; a 'rueful laugh' suggests a **near-comic moment, but instead panic ensues:** 'don't let them sister!'; a sense of **great distress** takes hold – he 'puffs his lips out' in pain; but there is **no real grief as he dies** – life is **cold, short and brutal.**

6. John Keats (2021)
'On First Looking into Chapman's Homer'

See	Hear	Feel
Speaker reflecting upon his 'travels' in the world of books and learning, **not a physical journey as such;** compares himself to an **astronomer** ('watcher of the skies') or an **explorer** ('Cortez ... with eagle eyes'); and is **thankful to the writer 'Chapman' for translating the work of Homer,** from Greek.	A **beautiful, rhythmic sonnet: fourteen lines that have a specific rhyme and rhythm;** heavily **metaphoric** words are used throughout: 'realms of gold', 'goodly states', 'kingdoms', 'western islands' **all refer to books he has read;** 'deep-brow'd Homer' indicates intelligence; 'ken' means vision or awareness; 'stout' means brave or strong.	**Reflective** and **descriptive** in the octet (first eight lines); speaks of his loyalty ('fealty') to learning and his gratitude/thanks to 'Chapman'; switches to **excitement** and **enthusiasm** in the sestet (last six lines) as he feels like a great explorer discovering the wonders of the world.

'La Belle Dame Sans Merci'

See	Hear	Feel
An unnamed narrator asks a knight what is wrong with him; he tells the story of meeting a beautiful lady – 'a faery's child' – they fell in love and they made 'sweet moan'. They go to her 'elfin grot', he kisses her (stanza 8) but he falls asleep; on awakening, she is gone; so he is left alone and 'palely loitering' as indicated at the start.	'La Belle Dame' is the beautiful lady; 'Sans Merci' means that she is 'without pity'; 'O what can ail thee' – **the language of a literary ballad;** other examples: thy brow; woe-begone; fast withereth; I love thee true; death-pale were they all; regular four-line stanzas – the fourth line is shorter and summarises each stanza.	**Curiosity:** What is wrong with this knight? **Intrigue:** Who is this mysterious lady? Where did she come from? **Excitement:** They head to her cave and the kiss each other – but what happened then? **Great disappointment:** The loss of his lady also means that his appearance fades; **love brings death and decay rather than happiness.**

7. Emily Dickinson (2020)
'I felt a Funeral, in my Brain'

See	Hear	Feel
Death scene; mourners walking back and forth; a **religious service** about to happen; music playing; lifting a **coffin**; heavy feet; a vision of **heaven**; a lonely **'solitary'** figure; at the moment of burial, a sudden shift – the **coffin falls downwards,** crashing through many levels; perhaps to **hell?** It is **unclear … a silence, then complete darkness.**	**Funeral music; mournful** tones; **treading** of feet; **drum beating** slowly; **creaking** as a coffin lifts; bell **ringing**; silence … **crashing and 'plunging'** downwards to a complete stop; then, a sense of **'nothingness'.**	A **sadness** 'in my Brain'; **anxiety** as mourners await the burial; the mind of the speaker is **'numb'** – perhaps with **fear**, perhaps unable to feel any more; **uncertainty** as the soul 'creaks'; leads to a more distinct **fear and absolute terror**; a 'Plank in Reason' breaks – the **solitary, utterly lonely soul finishes by 'knowing' something but we don't.**

'I heard a Fly buzz–when I died'

See	Hear	Feel
A **bare room,** in which the speaker is in the final moments of life; quiet, calm, serene, after a storm of some sort; others – **'The Eyes' – await the 'last rites'; God ('the King') is about to enter the room;** speaker makes a 'will' just before dying; then a fly **'interposes'** itself (gets in the way), buzzing around just as the speaker dies; **final image is of uncertainty, confusion;** the light 'fails' and the moment, and the speaker, are lost forever; **the fly becomes an eerie image of death.**	A **buzzing** fly disturbs the **peaceful,** sincere moment of the speaker's final breaths; other people also breathe heavily; all anticipate the arrival of a heavenly 'presence' at this moment; instead, a fly's buzzing dominates the scene; its **'uncertain stumbling Buzz'** creates a tension and **distaste in the room.**	A **startling and evocative opening line;** death, decay and dirt are all suggested; **contrasts the sense of power, protection** and security that the 'King' would bring; the entire scene is **'distracted'** by this apparently harmless fly; the fly renders the speaker **'powerless'**, unable to see/ understand anything.

8. Adrienne Rich (2020)
'Aunt Jennifer's Tigers'

See	Hear	Feel
Aunt Jennifer stitching; she creates a work of art – **tigers 'prancing' proudly in a 'topaz' and 'green' world;** unafraid of men who watch from beneath a tree; her hand **struggles with the task;** her ring **(wedding band) weighs her down;** then, an image of Aunt, **dead in her coffin;** she appears **terrified** – life has been difficult, filled with **'ordeals';** her **tigers live on in her work.**	Tigers **prancing** – moving playfully and powerfully; **'sleek chivalric certainty'** – they have style; **'finger fluttering'** – the task of stitching is tricky; **'massive weight'** – the wedding ring is a hindrance; **'ringed' and 'mastered' are excellent puns** – she has been 'surrounded' and overcome by oppressive forces; on the 'panel' of wool stitching, the tigers **prance** and are **proud; defiant sounds in these words.**	**Playfulness;** a natural and upbeat image of the natural world; **no fear of men;** contrasts with Aunt – she is **anxious** and perhaps **desperate to get her work of art completed;** marriage has weighed her down; but despite her death, her **proud defiance** is seen in the tigers; she is remembered forever in her work, despite her 'ordeals' of marriage.

'The Uncle Speaks in the Drawing Room'

See	Hear	Feel
First-person account; the **'Uncle' looks at a 'mob' of protesters;** looks down from a **balcony window** inside a large, **upper-class, long-established family home;** 'crystal vase and chandelier'; protesters hold **stones;** Uncle remembers previous events like this; **uses 'we' and 'us' to distinguish between classes** – We, the upper-class, or **'our kind';** 'glass-blowers' – skilled workers/craftsmen; 'Missile throwers' – **working class protesters.**	The mob **'standing sullen in the square';** **'bitter tones'** rhymes nicely with **'fingered stones'** – captures the **mood of the protesters;** 'follies' – foolishness or stupidity that will pass; glass, vase and chandelier all contrast with **'missiles'** – **potential for damage;** previous 'storms' – riots; **'grandsire'** – suggests fine breeding; **'us', 'we' and 'our kind' gives a lofty, elevated tone to the Uncle.**	**Disdain; dismissal; a sneering condescension** towards the protesters outside; **agitation; a sense of inequality or division;** there is a constant sense that the Uncle has an 'authority' over these matters and that the 'mob' must be resisted; no sense of discussion or communication; **he knows better;** he speaks for his people in their family mansion.

9. Elizabeth Bishop (2021)

'The Fish'

See	Hear	Feel
Fishing on a lake; fish with beautiful colours; big eyes; brown gills; green weeds; **five hooks still stuck in his jaw (important image)**; rainbow-coloured oil in the water; rusted orange; frightened look; **speaker lets the fish go free.**	'Tremendous fish'; 'grunting weight'; 'full-blown roses'; 'like medals with their ribbons' (simile); 'a five-haired beard of wisdom' (metaphor); 'I let the fish go' (narrative poem).	**Excitement** at first; but the speaker then describes the scene as if from a distance; **admiration** for the fish; changes to **sympathy** near the end – the speaker sees how **the fish has already suffered** but has overcome previous hardships and survived; so she lets him go.

'Filling Station'

See	Hear	Feel
Small rural filling station; dirty with **oil and grease everywhere**; a dog sits on a wicker sofa; the owner and his sons appear; **small glimpses of colour** – comics, a begonia flower, a doily (napkin), oil cans ('Esso').	'Oh but it is dirty'; 'Be careful with that match!'; 'several saucy greasy sons assist' **(alliteration)**; 'dirty dog, quite comfy' **(imagery)**; 'Why? Why? Why, oh why?' 'Somebody' is repeated – **hints at an absent figure, probably a mother.**	**Startling** beginning; **disgust** at first; **mocking** the dirtiness of it all; leads to **curiosity** and **intrigue**: what is this place? The importance of 'home', regardless of what it looks like, is hinted at. Concludes with **mystery**: who is the 'somebody'?

'The Prodigal'

See	Hear	Feel
Rotten pig-sty; filth everywhere; pigs watching the young man; he tries to bond with them; he has an alcohol problem; **sunrise suggests a new start**; but he remains '**exiled***'; farmer has little sympathy; pigs seem happy; he dreams of returning home someday, but not. yet. ***the state of being barred from entering one's home land; a punishment of some sort.**	'Prodigal' – a wasteful person; 'brown enormous odor' (pigs); 'plastered' (pun on drunkenness); 'sickening' for the man to live like this; 'the first star' – an image of fear as the darkness comes; 'Ark' – like Noah's ark, a safe place for the time being; 'shuddering insights' suggest the internal pain for the man.	**Disgust; dread; alienation; desperation** – especially to be accepted by anyone, even the pigs; a glint of **hope** each morning; replaced by a **fear of failure** with the arrival of evening; **powerlessness** – 'beyond his control'; **guilt**; concludes with a decision, an **assertiveness** – 'finally... to go home'.

10. Seamus Heaney (2021)
'A Constable Calls'

See	Hear	Feel
Local RUC Policeman visits the young speaker's home; bike and clothing described very closely; father makes his 'tillage returns' and **the policeman takes note**; a very 'officious' man; 'arithmetic and fear'; belt, baton case, polished holster and Domesday Book complete the **imposing picture**; speaker wonders if his father is being honest; he imagines the 'black hole' of a police cell; the constable leaves and **his bike 'ticks' away into the distance**.	'Mud-splasher', 'rubber cowl', 'fat black handle-grips', 'spud', 'dynamo', 'pedals', 'boot of the law' – **all communicate a big, awkward, uncomfortable presence**; 'pressure'; 'sweating'; 'heavy ledger'; bicycle; 'tick, tick, tick' is just like a bomb ready to explode.	'His' bicycle – he isn't referred to by his title – there is an **awkward discomfort at his presence; fascination** of the young speaker; turns to **fear as he thinks of the barracks**; there is a **'menacing'** tone as he cycles away – he will be back some day …

'The Underground'

See	Hear	Feel
Man and woman rushing to a concert; he is behind her as her buttons fall off in the rush; going 'underground' on the London Tube, they are late – it is **like a journey into the unknown, like their new marriage**; this is their honeymoon; one is leading the other but also one chases the other; 'damned if I look back' suggests **there is only one way to go from here – forwards**.	'Vaulted tunnel' – a journey into the deep; 'like a fleet god gaining on you' – **speaker enjoys the pursuit as a young lover**; 'moonlighting' suggests that they are involved in secretive or illegal activities by night; 'all attention for your step' – **the speaker realises that they are now together in all things**; they must look out for each other, like Hansel and Gretel.	**Tension, excitement and anxiety** all rolled into one in the first two stanzas; journeying through dark, crowded tunnels, racing to the theatre, but also anxious not to lose each other; **calm is restored near the end** but the speaker is still **anxious as to what their future together holds** – 'bared and tensed as I am'.

'A Call'

See	Hear	Feel
Speaker calling his elderly parents by phone; the mother goes to get the father from the garden; he is weeding; **very careful and meticulous*** – 'touching, inspecting, separating' – the speaker has time to wait and **listen to the clock ticking in the background** – like a clock ticking down to death; **realising our mortality, he almost says he loves his father when he does eventually speak.** *very close attention to detail	'"Hold on" she said' – contrasts with the clock ticking later – **time doesn't wait for anyone**; 'rueful' is an important word – both father and son share something of 'regret' in common – father regrets killing weeds, son regrets not having a more open relationship with him; the **irony*** here – the phone call is **mostly filled with silent thoughts and background noise.** *a contradiction between what is expected and what actually happens	**Uplifting, positive, everyday conversation between mother and son**; admiration for the father's **dedication and hard-working attitude**; but great **tension: to share his feelings or hold back?** 'I nearly said I loved him' carries the main message of the poem: **we only have a short time on earth in which to express our love.**

11. William Wordsworth (2020)
'She dwelt among the untrodden ways'

See	Hear	Feel
An **ambiguous lady named 'Lucy'**; her beauty becomes apparent; wandering along an isolated path; **a small river** ('springs of Dove'); she is unknown to many; **flowers, mossy stone, stars, sky – Romantic imagery;** she is an **image from the past – she is currently dead;** this strongly affects the speaker – she is **lost to him forever.**	**Regular rhythm and rhyme throughout**; almost **'musical'** quality to the stanzas; 'dwelt' – past tense; 'untrodden' – remote, isolated; 'violet by a mossy stone' (**metaphor**); 'fair as a star' (**simile**); 'ceased to be' (**euphemism for death**); 'oh' – strongly emphasises the emotional effect of her death.	**Dream-like reflections; mournful** – nobody was there to praise her, very few who loved her; a sense of **contradiction** – such a wonderful lady is gone – she **'shines' in her own way;** a unique individual who is sadly no longer here.

'It is a beauteous evening, calm and free'

See	Hear	Feel
A mixture of **religious and natural imagery throughout;** it is evening time; 'adoration' (prayer); sunset and sea depict heaven and the 'mighty Being' is God; 'Abraham's bosom all the year'; a child, walking with the speaker; she is almost 'divine' – **God is with her, even if the speaker isn't or has not been up to this moment.**	**14-line sonnet** – a distinct rhyming scheme (ABBA, ABBA, CDE, DEC); **'beauteous'** – a more profound form of beauty; a calm conclusion to the day; 'holy time' – a religious or spiritual experience; 'quiet as a nun' – an amusing **simile;** tranquillity; **'broods'** – heaven looks over its creation; 'mighty Being' – **metaphor for God;** thunder – the 'power' of God; untouched – innocent, pure; 'Abraham's bosom' – a **metaphor;** she is close to divinity.	**Intimacy; a sense of closeness between the speaker and the child;** a 'sacred' moment, given the numerous religious references; **nature is powerful and potentially threatening;** but the child is innocent and 'at one' with nature; great **tenderness** from the speaker towards her; a **celebratory poem.**

From *The Prelude*: 'Skating'

See	Hear	Feel
A perfect winter scene; cottages, a village near at sunset; **young boys,** like horses or a pack of hounds, **enjoy skating across ice;** 'not a voice was idle' – they thoroughly enjoy it; the **speaker retires to a 'silent bay' away from the others** – a key image of Romantic poetry is the **'isolated' poet in solitude, contemplating the natural world;** the passing of time, youth and old age; as they spin on the ice, so does the earth, and time passes.	**Brilliant sounds throughout:** clock 'tolled six'; young boys shouting excitedly; horses galloping; the hiss of the skates on ice; hunting horns blowing; dogs yelping; echoes come from the hills ('the precipices rang aloud'); the ice on the trees 'tinkles' – like a Christmas scene; **then there is silence, as the speaker retires to the solitude of the bay;** the earth rotates silently by day ('diurnal') and the poet sits in contemplation.	'an alien sound of melancholy' – **this is the key to the poem; a type of sadness 'not unnoticed' grips the speaker half way through;** despite the excitement, joy and exuberance of youth, it all passes in time; however, **the speaker appreciates the tranquillity of this moment of reflection;** he also appreciates the wonder of the natural world, taking the time to do so – a key idea in Romantic poetry.

12. D. H. Lawrence (2020)
'Baby-Movements II: "Trailing Clouds"'

See	Hear	Feel
Lines 1–7 – the baby is described like a **honey-bee, clinging to a flower**; clinging to the speaker – most likely the poet himself, speaking as if he is a 'mother'. Lines 8–10 – the baby is a 'burden' that **depends entirely on the mother for life.** Lines 11–16 – the baby now seems quite heavy, as if **mother and baby are weighed down by some 'weariness'.**	'drenched, drowned bee'; 'numb and heavy'; 'laid laughterless on her cheek'; even though the scene is **silent,** we can sense **some great upheaval has occurred;** 'sways ... like sorrowful, storm-heavy boughs ... storm bruised young leaves'; **heaviness and weariness suggest a great strain** in being the parent of this child.	Tremendous sense of **connection and dependency** all through; love is also very much evident as the child 'So clings to me' and also 'swings to my lullaby'; 'burden' and 'downwards' are two key words that suggest the feeling of being **overwhelmed by the challenges of being a parent;** weariness also suggests how tiring and demanding this role is.

'Humming-Bird'

See	Hear	Feel
Speaker imagines a time long ago; the hummingbird survived down through all the centuries through its **fierce determination** – 'went whizzing through the slow, vast, succulent stems'; it 'flashed ahead of creation,' surviving despite its small size and lack of flowers to provide nectar; maybe **we have underestimated a creature like the humming-bird,** looking through 'the wrong end of the telescope of Time'.	'Primeval-dumb' – **a time before history, long ago;** the humming-bird 'raced down avenues' while everything else moved so slowly; the 'heave' of matter is so slow, while the 'whizzing' bird flies onwards; 'jabbing, terrifying monster'; the humming-bird **sounds like a giant dinosaur;** 'Luckily for us': the speaker remarks that humans are lucky that his imaginative story is not true.	**Light-hearted descriptions;** not to be taken literally; reflective **imaginative thoughts** by the speaker; 'I believe' is not a scientific fact but just an imaginative thought; **humorous ending** – 'luckily for us' the humming-bird is small and harmless.

13. Sylvia Plath (2021)
'Poppies in July'

See	Hear	Feel
A field of poppies; images of hell; flickering flames; a hand in the fire; a mouth that is bleeding; red skirts; 'opiates' – the mind-altering substances in drugs; **images of sickness:** 'nausea' and suffering ('marry a hurt like that'); a glass jar or container, holding this 'poison' that **makes the speaker dull and lifeless.**	'Little' – suggests **something delicate or harmless but NOT in this case;** 'it exhausts me' – the speaker sounds **worn out, anxious, depressed maybe?;** 'a mouth just bloodied' – domestic violence maybe?; 'If I could bleed or sleep!' – **a strange question; perhaps looking for a relief from some great anxiety;** 'dulling', 'stilling', 'colourless': all these words indicate **a numbness and a longing for release,** perhaps from life itself.	Initially **curious;** lots of questions; wondering about the power of the poppies; **intrigued** by their unusual properties; 'A mouth just bloodied:' a change in direction – **much more violent suggestions; anxious questions** in stanza 5 – leads to desperate pleading in stanza 6; a **disturbing and frightening conclusion** with the word 'colourless' – there is **no energy or enthusiasm** left in the speaker; she is deflated.

'Child'

See	Hear	Feel
Newborn baby; clear-eyed and innocent; colours and experiences from **early childhood;** flowers and animals; but things **change with the word 'Pool';** the 'darkness' it hints at is **frightening;** 'troublous wringing of hands' is a **famous image of anxiety and deep distress;** the 'ceiling without a star' is a **life for the baby without its mother.**	'Clear eye'; 'absolutely beautiful thing'; 'colour and ducks'; 'zoo of the new'; all combine to capture brilliantly the **sounds of a wonderfully happy new mother and child;** 'Little' – the word is placed on its own; **the child is vulnerable, on many levels;** 'troublous wringing of hands' – things change dramatically; **mother is very anxious, and despairing.**	**Pride; pure love and adoration;** the speaker wants the child to only have pleasant experiences; **excitement** at the possibilities to come – the 'zoo of the new'; **great ambition** for the child – 'grand and classical' images; but the final stanza is **shocking and heart-breaking in its honesty** – the speaker committed suicide two weeks later.

Sample questions and answers – Prescribed Poetry

On the following page is a typical question with sample answers on one of the poets prescribed. Remember that four of the poems you work on will be printed on the exam paper. Spend time reading the questions and the poems before making a choice and beginning to write.

CHILD OF OUR TIME
(*for Aengus*)

Yesterday I knew no lullaby
But you have taught me overnight to order
This song, which takes from your final cry
Its tune, from your unreasoned end its reason,
Its rhythm from the discord of your murder
Its motive from the fact you cannot listen.

We who should have known how to instruct
With rhymes for your waking, rhythms for your sleep,
Names for the animals you took to bed,
Tales to distract, legends to protect,
Later an idiom for you to keep
And living, learn, must learn from you, dead,

To make our broken images rebuild
Themselves around your limbs, your broken
Image, find for your sake whose life our idle
Talk has cost, a new language. Child
Of our time, our times have robbed your cradle.
Sleep in a world your final sleep has woken.

Eavan Boland, 17 May 1974

Sample Questions

1.   (a) From your reading of the above poem, describe the poet's
         reaction to the child's murder. Support your answer with
         reference to the poem.   **(10)**

     (b) Describe, in your own words, the childhood experiences the
         poet writes about in lines eight, nine and ten of the poem.   **(10)**

     (c) Based on your study of 'Child of Our Time', explain what you
         hink the poet is saying in the last line of the poem.   **(10)**

SAMPLE ANSWER (A)

The poet is shocked and saddened at the murder of the
child. She says that 'we who should have known how'
without saying who the 'we' is. This is an interesting part
of the poem. It is as if the death is so shocking that

all people, whoever they may be, should share in the shock of seeing a picture of a dead baby in a city like Dublin. The phrase 'our times have robbed your cradle' is saddening, as again the word 'our' stands out, to suggest that we are all involved, in some way, for the death of the baby. Together, these two quotes suggest that the poet is shocked and saddened. But Boland manages to avoid putting the blame directly on any known person or group, even though at the time, everybody knew who was really responsible. This shows how a poem can put into words the strong feelings that emerge at a time like this, without causing further outrage.

(164 words)

EXAMINER'S ASSESSMENT

The candidate chooses two appropriate words to base the answer upon and then elaborates with quotation. This should score full marks as it addresses the question directly and coherently.

MARKS AWARDED

6 + 4 = 10/10 (O1 Grade)

SAMPLE ANSWER (B)

The poet paints a picture associated with childhood happiness and innocence in these lines. The particular words to notice are 'rhymes', 'tales' and 'legends', all associated with telling children stories, often as a way of teaching lessons or helping them sleep. It is impossible to see these images without seeing a mother, father or relative caring for the young child, at a very tender and innocent time in their life. This becomes particularly sad when later in the poem we see that 'sleep' becomes a metaphor for the death of the child in the bomb, the 'final sleep'. I think Boland was using lines 8–10 to prepare us for the final line. This is a good way of creating powerful ideas in the reader's head.

(126 words)

EXAMINER'S ASSESSMENT

The candidate takes an excellent approach to this question – by explaining lines 8–10 in their own words, it then allows them to see these lines in the context of the poem as a whole. This is explained in the second part of the answer and overall, despite being brief, this is a top-class response for 10 marks.

MARKS AWARDED

6 + 4 = 10/10 (O1 Grade)

SAMPLE ANSWER (C)

First of all, there is an interesting contrast between 'sleep' and 'woken' in the final line. This can be taken literally, as we can be woken from our sleep by a loud noise like a bomb. But I think the metaphoric meaning is more powerful and is probably what Boland had in mind. The sleep of the child is a death – a final sleep that the child should not have to experience so young. This causes the rest of us to wake up – we are 'woken' into the harsh reality of terrorism and murder on the streets of our capital city. This line can be read like a warning of some sort, in that we all need to 'wake up' to how awful the world is becoming. This is what I think the final line means.

(137 words)

EXAMINER'S ASSESSMENT

The candidate identifies the contrast in the last line and explains this fully thereafter. Explaining the difference between the literal and the metaphoric indicates a good grasp of the meaning and deserves high marks.

MARKS AWARDED

6 + 4 = 10/10 (O1 Grade)

Question 2: 20 Marks/15 Minutes

Question 2, worth 20 marks, is a little different.

- You may be asked to state what you liked/disliked about the entire poem.
- You may be required to use the poem as an inspiration to create an imaginative response.
- You may be asked to go beyond the words of the poem and create your own situation.

For example, you could be asked to write one of these:

- **Letter to the poet.**
- **Diary of one of the characters.**
- **Describe a film based on the poem.**
- **Would you like to be in this place/situation?**
- **What would appeal to/annoy you most about this poem?**
- **Continue the story outlined in the poem.**

Note: In recent years, students have had **three options** on this question, so as usual, read all options carefully and make a sound decision.

Sample Question

2. (ii) In your opinion, is the poem 'Child of Our Time' still relevant today?
          Explain your response, supporting your answer with reference
          to the poem.   (20)

SAMPLE ANSWER (2) (ii)

I think that 'Child of Our Time' is still relevant today, but
maybe it is more relevant to events in the international
world, rather than in Ireland. We are lucky that we
do not have terrorists on the go in Ireland and we
don't have the Troubles anymore, which provides the
background to this poem. We live in a country where the
relationship between Ireland and England has become
friendlier. So instead of just thinking of this poem as
being about a bombing in Ireland, we could apply it to
anywhere in the world where children are killed for no
apparent reason, especially by terrorists or bombers, or
simply those who spread hate.

'You cannot listen' is a good starting point. A lot of
conflict arises because people do not listen to each other
and are only interested in their own point of view. It gets
even worse when social media is used to promote killing,
bombing and terrorism. When people are killed, or if
they take their own lives, it is too late to 'listen' then, so I
think this line is still relevant.

'Our times have robbed your cradle' is another line that
is relevant today. When we see news stories from war
zones today, we often see children and mothers left
without homes or without support. We continue to
'rob the cradle' by making the future so dark for these
children. We are also robbing their cradle through global
warming and pollution, caused by 'our times' full of 'idle
talk' by world leaders. When I read this poem again, I see
that it can clearly apply to the world today.

(276 words)

EXAMINER'S ASSESSMENT

The candidate displays a level of reflection in the answer which indicates a clear
engagement with the question. It reads like a very short personal essay and is
well-expressed in clear language. Two main points are made and references are
included. A high-scoring response.

MARKS AWARDED

12 + 8 = 20/20 (O1 Grade)

9 Time-keeping and Revision Checklist

aims
- To learn an efficient **time schedule** for the exam papers.
- To develop an effective **checklist for revision**.

Time Schedule for the Exam

Students frequently wonder how much they should write in the exam. Rather than thinking in terms of lines or pages, a better question is: **how much can I write in the time allowed?** If the Comprehension B question should take 35 minutes, consider how much you can plan and write in that time. The only real way to find out is to practise answers yourself. Follow the suggested outline below. It takes you through both papers chronologically to show you how your time should be divided.

exam focus

These times are approximate. The goal is to answer the questions as best you can in the time allowed.

Paper 1: Wednesday morning

9.30 a.m.   Begin by reading the entire paper – slowly. Take 10 minutes to read and choose your questions.

9.40 a.m.   Comprehension A (1, 2, 3) carries 50 marks. Allow 35 minutes.

10.15 a.m.   Begin Comprehension B. It carries 50 marks, so allow 35 minutes. Take 5 minutes to plan your piece and 30 minutes to write it.

10.50 a.m.   Begin your Composition plan. Think broadly and try to get your opening and conclusion sorted first. Take 10 minutes to plan your composition.

11.00 a.m. Start the Composition. It carries 100 marks. You now have 80 minutes to finish the exam. You should use 10 of these 80 minutes to go back over your work. Do not leave early unless you are totally satisfied with your efforts.

12.20 p.m. Paper 1 ends.

After Paper 1 you should rest, rest, rest!

Paper 2: Thursday afternoon

2.00 p.m. Begin by quickly indentifying your: Single Text (one out of nine); preferred Comparative mode (one out of two); and preferred Poem (one out of four). Read only the questions relevant to your chosen texts. Mark them clearly on your exam paper. Allow 10 minutes for all of this.

The exam is not a sprint! There are no marks for finishing early.

2.10 p.m. Single Text Question 1 (a, b and c). There are 30 marks here, so allow 30 minutes.

2.40 p.m. Single Text Question 2. There are 30 marks here, so allow 25 minutes. Make a short plan to help you answer this question.

3.05 p.m. Comparative Study. There are two questions: one with 30 marks and another with 40 marks. Aim to write more on the second question. Allow 65 minutes in total.

4.10 p.m. Unseen Poetry. Read the poem slowly at least three times. Pause. Answer the two 10-mark questions. Write quickly here. You have only 20 minutes.

Time always flies in exam situations, so don't dwell too much on your work. Check over everything once at the end of the exam.

4.30 p.m. Prescribed Poetry. Read your chosen poem twice. You now have 50 minutes to finish the exam. Answer the Prescribed Poetry questions in 45 minutes and leave yourself 5 minutes at the end to look back at your answers.

5.20 p.m. English Leaving Certificate exam ends.

Revision Checklist

Refer to the checklists below in preparation for your exam. Relevant chapters are listed as a reminder.

Paper 1 checklist

- Different **Language Genres**: See Chapters 2, 3, 4 and 5.
  - Informative language
  - Narrative language
  - Persuasive language
  - Argumentative language
  - Aesthetic language
- Two basic writing **styles** (and their variations): See Chapters 4 and 5.
  - Story
  - Discussion
- Do you prefer telling stories or having discussions? See Chapter 5.
- Do you understand the difference between a story and a personal essay? See Chapter 5.

Paper 2 checklist

- The name and correct spelling of the **title** and **author** of your **Single Text**. See Chapter 6.
- The **storyline** of your Single Text. You must know this in great detail. See Chapter 6.
- The main **characters** of your Single Text and their major **traits**. See Chapter 6.
- The **major themes** or issues raised by your Single Text. See Chapter 6.
- The names and correct spellings of the **texts** for your **Comparative Study**. See Chapter 7.
- Your favourite or '**anchor**' **text** for the Comparative Study. Also, your least favourite, if you have studied three. See Chapter 7.
- The three **modes** for the Comparative Study. See Chapter 7.
- The **key moments** in your chosen Comparative Texts. See Chapter 7.
- The twelve most important **terms** in poetry. See Chapter 8.
- The value of understanding **feelings** in poetry and being able to write about them in your answers. See Chapter 8.

General checklist

- The length of **time** that you can spend on each section of the exam. See the time guide above.
- The **length** that you expect your answers to be (in terms of pages or paragraphs).
- The importance of **structure** in your exam answers. Compositions will have defined features, as suggested in the questions. Paper 2 answers should follow the formula: **point–quote–support**.
- **Spelling and mechanics** count for **10%** of all marks. See the marking scheme in Chapter 2.
- **60%** of the marks is for **what** you write and **40%** is for **how** you write it. See the marking scheme in Chapter 2.
- Remember: exam success is mostly about **preparation**, with a little **perspiration** and some **inspiration** on the day!

If you are sure of all of the above, then you are well prepared for the Leaving Certificate English exam. However, a final word of warning: even the most seasoned English teacher will tell you that a certain amount of the exam is determined by the inspiration that a student experiences on the day. This cannot be taught. So, prepare well and do lots of work; then hope things go your way on the day!

Each student must do their very best with what they bring to the exam. The bottom line is to trust in your own ability. Generally, when you have worked really hard, you do reap rewards on the day of the exam.

Good luck!

Below is a glossary of useful words and phrases, many of which appear throughout this book.

Aesthetics are associated with beauty. Aesthetics are an essential aspect of creative writing.

Alliteration occurs when words that begin with the same letter are used close together for a sound effect.

Anchor text: This is the text that you know best from your Comparative Study. You will use this text as a base for your answers.

Argumentative language is logical language that aims to prove a point.

Atmosphere is a word used to describe the feelings generated by a piece of writing or suggested by a picture.

Audience: Those who experience a text or drama; people who will read your written work.

Bias is the state of favouring one side or having a strong preference.

Brainstorming is the process of jotting down all of your thoughts related to a specific issue.

Clarity means being clear and certain in your writing.

Cliché: A phrase that is tired, overused and lacks originality.

Climax is the moment of highest tension in a text, film or drama.

Coherence means making logical sense from beginning to end.

Commentary is writing that comments on or gives an opinion about some other work. See the Examiner's Assessments on Sample Answers throughout the text.

Composition: This is the second section of Paper 1; a piece of written work composed by a writer.

Comprehension means 'understanding'. Also, it is the name of the first question on Paper 1. It tests your ability to respond to questions on a given text extract.

Confidence is the sum total of one's feeling about oneself. Having confidence means having belief in one's abilities.

Diary: A day-to-day, informal or personal account of events. It is usually in written form.

Discussion: To have a discussion means to talk about an issue, to declare an opinion and to share it. Discussion appears throughout the book.

Emotive language is language that gives rise to emotions and strong reactions.

Format means the form that a piece of writing takes, what it looks like and how it is structured. Examination of format appears throughout the book.

Genre means a type of work. Texts can be classified into different genres, e.g. comedy, tragedy, horror.

Hero: The main character in a text. Sometimes heroes have a fatal flaw or weakness (hubris) that brings about personal tragedy.

Heroine: This is a female hero.

Hyperbole is gross exaggeration or overstatement.

Imagery means pictures generated in the mind by the written word.

Informative language is language that gives factual information.

Mechanics: The mechanics of language include spelling, grammar and punctuation. Mechanics are discussed throughout the book.

Metaphor is a colourful, creative description that is not to be understood literally. Metaphors are often found in poetry.

Metre is the beat or rhythm in a line of poetry.

Modes of Comparison are the headings under which you must compare texts in the Comparative Study.

Mood is the feeling generated by a text.

Narrative language is language used to tell a story.

Objective: An objective is something to aim for. 'Objective' has another meaning: to be objective means to be unbiased, to see things from all sides. The word 'objective' appears throughout the text.

Onomatopoeia occurs when the meaning of the word closely matches its sound, e.g. fizz, pop, crunch.

Personification occurs when non-human or inanimate objects are described as if they had human characteristics.

Persuasive language is language that tries to convince an audience of a particular viewpoint.

Planning is a vital aspect of writing any answer. Learn the art of being prepared! The notion of planning appears throughout the text.

Pun: This is a play on words. It occurs when words can be understood in more than one way.

Purpose is the reason behind something. You must always have a clear purpose when you are writing. Purpose appears throughout the book.

Quotation: The exact spoken words of a character in a text. Quotation appears throughout the text.

Register is a mixture of tone, vocabulary and purpose. Register is a vital characteristic that determines the success of your writing.

Relationships are an essential ingredient in all texts. Consider how people interact with each other in any text you study.

Resolution is the ending of a text.

Rhetorical question: This occurs when a question is asked and the answer is not given because it is either obvious or the questioner wants the audience to think and reflect.

Rhyme occurs when words that have similar sounds are used together for poetic effect.

Sarcasm is a scornful tone in writing and acting that pokes fun and can injure feelings.

Simile is a comparison that uses 'as' or 'like' to make a description more colourful.

Slang is low and somewhat vulgar forms of expression.

Social setting is the time and place in which a text is located.

Stanza is a collection of lines of poetry.

Statement is something written or spoken and usually presented as fact. Statements appear throughout the book.

Structure is how paragraphs and essays are shaped and put together. Structure is discussed throughout the book.

Syntax is the order in which words appear in a sentence.

Tension is a build-up of uncertainty, excitement or fear during a text.

Theme is the main issue raised or discussed by a text. It is more than just the plot or story.

Tone is the 'sound' of writing and the feeling suggested in its delivery. Tone creates a mood.

Verbiage is excessive language use, or writing that tries to sound sophisticated but isn't.

Verbose: To be verbose is to overuse language and sophisticated vocabulary that actually carries little genuine meaning.

Villain: The 'bad guy' in a text. Villains can be male or female.

Visuals are pictures, photographs, film stills, etc.

Vocabulary is a person's choice of words or level of language. Vocabulary is mentioned throughout the book.

Waffle is words that do not mean very much in the context of an exam answer.